SHA

in the
Global
Family of Faith

SHARING GIFTS
in the
Global
Family of Faith

One Church's Experiment

Pakisa K. Tshimika & Tim Lind

Photographs by Merle Good

Published in cooperation with Mennonite World Conference

Intercourse, PA 17534
800/762-7171
www.goodbks.com

Sharing Gifts in the Global Family of Faith is published in cooperation with Mennonite World Conference.

Mennonite World Conference (MWC) is an international fellowship of Christian churches who trace their beginning to the 16th-century Radical Reformation in Europe, particularly to the Anabaptist movement. Today, more than 1,200,000 believers belong to this faith family; at least 55 percent are African, Asian, or Latin American.

MWC represents 87 Mennonite and Brethren in Christ national churches from 48 countries on five continents.

Creating a "space" is a primary ministry of MWC — where member churches experience communion, interdependence, solidarity, and mutual accountability. MWC provides occasions and networks, publications and exchanges where Mennonites and Brethren in Christ can experience fellowship and be encouraged to live and act more faithfully.

MWC intends to serve as a "global congregation," believing that the church is a worldwide body where people of different cultures and nations are "no longer strangers . . . but members of God's household . . . " (Ephesians 2:19)

MWC's headquarters are in Strasbourg, France. For more information, visit its website at www.mwc-cmm.org.

Scripture quotations are from the *New Revised Standard Version* of the Bible, copyright © 1989, 1995 by the Division of Christian Education of the National Council of the Churches of Christ in the United States of America, and are used by permission. All rights reserved.

All photographs on both covers and throughout the text are by Merle Good.

Design by Dawn J. Ranck

SHARING GIFTS IN THE GLOBAL FAMILY OF FAITH:
ONE CHURCH'S EXPERIMENT
Copyright © 2003 by Good Books, Intercourse, PA 17534
International Standard Book Number: 1-56148-387-7
Library of Congress Catalog Card Number: 2003049111

Library of Congress Cataloging-in-Publication Data
Tshimika, Pakisa K.
   Sharing gifts in the global family of faith : one church's experiment / Pakisa K. Tshimika & Tim Lind ; photographs by Merle Good.
      p. cm.
"Published in cooperation with Mennonite World Conference."
   ISBN 1-56148-387-7
   1. Gifts--Religious aspects--Christianity. 2. Sharing--Religious aspects--Christianity. I. Lind, Tim. II. Mennonite World Conference. III. Title.
   BR115.G54T79 2003
   289.7'09--dc21   2003049111

Table of Contents

1.
In the Beginning

Open my eyes, so that I may behold wondrous things . . .

(Psalm 119:18)

Beginning is a relative thing. There are always roots, and before roots seeds, and before seeds, the plants from which the seeds came, and so forth. For the two of us who were asked to give shape and direction to a Global Gift Sharing program, we think of the beginning in Harare, Zimbabwe, in December of 1998. The venue was a rather Spartan church guesthouse/conference center on the outskirts of town. Pakisa and I were lodged together in a room with two narrow beds and a wooden bedside stand, with a bathroom down the hall.

We met there for several days—at times just the two of us, and at times with several members of our executive committee—to plan how this venture in highlighting and nurturing the gifts of the churches would work. At the same time we began the process of trying to find some common understandings about the idea of gift sharing, what gifts are, where they come from, and how they should be used. We have been learning about gift sharing ever since.

The strategy which evolved from that initial meeting was to visit each member conference, first in Africa, then in Latin

3

America and Asia, and finally in Europe and North America, holding workshops to teach and encourage the sharing of gifts in the church. We anticipated that out of these encounters would emerge a worldwide inventory of diverse gifts which could be shared among churches. More importantly, it was the hope of our organization, Mennonite World Conference, that Global Gift Sharing would encourage a new vision within the churches about the gifts God has given us and how we use them.

We began this work among the African churches, then proceeded to Latin America and Asia, for several reasons. First, Pakisa and I were both living in Africa at the time, and our combined knowledge of the African churches was probably greater than of the churches of any other region. But more important, our experiences gave us an awareness of some of the diversity of gifts within the African churches, and we felt we could envision how the program would work there.

Over the following two years we made visits to each of the conferences in Africa, meeting with about 350 people in 13 workshops in 10 different countries. During that time, and continuing with our work in Latin America and Asia where we trained facilitators from the churches to do the workshops, we learned many things about gifts. We also received many different kinds of gifts from the people we met. This book is our attempt to share some of what we have learned—about gifts, about the churches, about sharing, and about God.

In this book we occasionally use the terms "North" and "South" to refer to Europe and North America, on the one hand, and Asia, Latin America and Africa on the other. These terms are classifications which, like many categories, are often awkward as well as literally inaccurate. It has been said in the context of biology that the variety within a given species is often greater than the variety between two species. This is true with the terms North and South. In addition, such terms quickly create stereotypes that go well beyond the geographical meanings, and which can prevent rather than facilitate communication and creative reflection.

The churches throughout the world are infinitely more complex than the terms North and South would suggest. In order for the Northern/Southern classification to have useful meaning, we have tried to use it sparingly in this book.

Where We Come From

Pakisa Tshimika (Pa-kee'-sa Cha-mee'-ka): I experienced two worldviews of gifts and gift sharing during Christmastime when I was a child in Africa. On Christmas Eve our church would organize a pageant where the whole Christmas story would be told in a very detailed and dramatic manner. I remember that at the end of the pageant, missionaries passed out soap and salt to all the people who came for the program. In school as well as in Sunday school, we were given coloring books and pencils. We did not have to give anything to our teachers in return, and I don't remember people giving anything to the missionaries who were passing out soap or salt. I learned that there were two categories of people—those who gave and those who received.

Pakisa Tshimika

However, the story did not end there. Soon after the church program on Christmas day, people would get together to share meals. Two or three families would bring food together and share what they had with each other. I learned the other lesson—we all have something to contribute in a relationship, and the principle of the "haves" and the "have-nots" does not always hold. I grew up living with this tension of the two worldviews throughout my childhood and adolescent and college years.

Tim Lind: Growing up as one of six children in a family of modest means, I can't remember learning specifically about sharing. It was just always there in very practical ways—the way the food got divided up at the table, the way clothes were passed from one child to another, deciding who would share bedrooms and beds with whom. And in the day-to-day relationships with my brothers and sister, "taking turns" was a key concept in the vocabulary of sharing. I can call up countless scenes of dis-

Tim Lind

cussions among us about "whose turn" it was. Of course these "discussions" were often self-interested ("It's my turn!"), but there were also clearly acknowledged limits to self-interest. Somehow it was always understood—there was never the least question—that within the family, the total space belonged to everyone, and it just wasn't acceptable or even fun, to accumulate or possess at the expense of your brother or sister. In a family you learn naturally, and repeatedly, that keeping things for yourself isolates you and in the long term isn't healthy.

PT: When I worked in public health and community development in poor settings, I found it almost impossible to overcome the notion of "haves" and "have-nots" among those I worked with. It made sense that many people considered me a "have" because I was on the giving side. I had studied in some of the best schools the world has to offer. I had a good job and was being paid regularly, while many around me would go for several months without being paid. Furthermore, I had a nice house and did not have to worry about whether I'd have food from one day to another. But from time to time someone from a village nearby would bring me a stalk of bananas. "I was thinking of you and how you like bananas so I brought you some," my friend would say to me. Nothing was expected in return, and this person did not care about what kind of money I made. These people knew that I liked bananas and they just wanted to share them with me.

TL: My wife and I spent most of the 1970s, the "great development decade," in Africa, working in different countries in the planning and administration of a variety of relief and community development programs. It was a heady time, and the air was filled with the energy of sure solutions. But increasingly the promises of development seemed hollow and its premises suspect. It seemed to me that there were too many parts of the paradigm that were untrue, ineffective, and inconsistent with the faith story.

It was in 1982 that a colleague sent me an excerpt of a book by Lewis Hyde titled *The Gift*. The book examines the role that gifts, both material objects and immaterial talents and inspirations, play in our lives. It contrasts the market economy, where increase is achieved by hoarding or saving, with what Hyde calls the "gift economy," in which increase comes through circulation or spending. While the market economy isolates us and makes us independent of each other, the whole purpose of the gift economy is to build relationships, to connect us one to the other.

I have been thinking, reading, and studying about this metaphor ever since. It seems to me it is a more fruitful way, and one more consistent with biblical faith, of thinking about how people in different situations can interact with each other.

PT: When I was called to be part of a team to develop a project on gifts and gift sharing, I wondered what kind of contribution I had to bring to the project. Mine has been this tension between the two worldviews which surrounded me in my childhood and later in my professional environment. The church I grew up in did not help me in dealing with this tension. I seemed to be living in two worlds. In one, I was taught about the hierarchy of gifts—preachers, evangelists, prophets, and those who can perform miracles, seemingly more important than a woman who is a member who prepares meals for church gatherings or a carpenter, also a member, who builds roofs for our churches and schools. In my family and other social settings outside the church, I was taught that we all have something to contribute and each gift is important in our society. This tension became an asset as we developed the framework for our seminars, as well as when we started conducting workshops on gifts and gift sharing in churches around the world.

TL: Pakisa and I had met a number of times over the years, in Kinshasa, Congo, and elsewhere. We were both involved in church-related development work, and I guess we knew each other by reputation. But what was before us now was something quite different. The two of us were to take an idea about sharing gifts within the worldwide church—which had been spelled out in two or three sparse paragraphs by a Mennonite

World Conference committee—develop it into a global program, and implement it. Furthermore, we were to do this on a part-time basis, with both of us formally employed by other agencies, and we were to do it together—two Mennonite laypersons, an African who had spent many years in North America and a North American who had spent many years in Africa.

And what did we know about gifts? What expertise did we bring to this subject? Very little, in fact. Neither of us is a theologian or pastor or philosopher or sociologist. We did share a strong commitment to the church, long experience working with mission and service organizations of the church, primarily in Africa, and a deep belief in the value and connectedness of all human beings.

PT: So what did we learn from this project? Writing about everything we learned would be more than this book is intended to cover. In summary I would say that the process is as important as the end product, we experienced personal growth, and we have had the joy of self-discovery. Our first thought was that we would end up with a very nice document with tables and detailed information listing all the gifts and resources found in each church we visited. But soon after the first two workshops we realized that the process of gift sharing discernment was becoming as important as the end product. People who attended the workshops talked about how their views of gifts and gift sharing were changing as we continued the discussions.

A comment made by one of the participants in a workshop got my attention. He said that in his studies in a theological school he was never challenged regarding his view of gifts and gift sharing. He remarked that his new understanding of gifts was also influencing his view of leadership in the church. His

We've had many light moments as we've traveled around talking with churches about gifts. We remember how in Guatemala City, after we had been meeting for several days with a group of Latin American facilitators, they admitted to us during a coffee break that before we met, when we were corresponding with them as "Tim and Pakisa," they had all assumed that we were husband and wife.

comments were echoed by many more participants from other settings we visited in the course of the project. On one occasion we brought churches from two countries together for the workshop. Although from neighboring countries, these two churches had never done anything together and never realized how much they had in common. In another church our workshop was the first time, as far as participants could remember, that lay people, clergy, and men and women of all ages were brought together to discuss an important aspect of church life, in this case gift discernment.

Church members also found through these workshops an opportunity to discuss other matters affecting the church. Issues related to youth, women in leadership, communication, church stewardship, and a sense of isolation are among those that were raised in each workshop. Although we did not anticipate discussing these subjects, participants found this forum to be an appropriate setting to air these other concerns of major importance to their churches.

Another aspect that became clear to us is the importance of the sense of belonging to a larger family of faith. One of the churches had been excluded from global fellowship due to internal conflict. They had since dealt with the conflict, and we were visiting them for a workshop on the Global Gift

Sharing Project. We remember vividly that as the session ran on into the middle of the night we had the opportunity to tell them that their church had been restored to the global fellowship because the reason they were excluded did not exist anymore. The leader stopped us and requested that we spend time in prayer and singing to God because their church was once again a part of the global family.

TL: What strikes me when I look back on our experiences to date is the wealth of diversity one finds from church to church, from country to country. Sometimes I have felt that *difference* is just another word for *gift*. And once we start thinking deliberately about gifts and differences, we see them everywhere—different ways of singing, of worshiping, different ways of being a family, of being a church, different ways of making a living, different ways of dressing, of cooking and eating, different languages and accents. Difference is such a beautiful thing; how ironic it seems that often we allow our differences—our gifts—to divide us and keep us apart, as though it would be better if we were all the same! How sad it is that the ugliest acts in human history have been committed because of these beautiful differences.

PT: The gift sharing process also provided excellent occasion for personal growth. It is one thing to conduct a workshop on gifts and gift sharing and to talk about wonderful concepts and the different biblical models of gifts and gift sharing. But it is another thing to practice and live these ideals. During the workshops we discussed how one gift tends to encourage another. During our own work we discovered how Tim and I needed each other to accomplish our tasks. I needed Tim's critical mind, writing skills, and wide network of relationships from his previous international work experience. Tim is not pushy in his approach but he is well organized. He is also very

There is nothing quite like watching people discover their gifts.

good at keeping in touch with all the people we met along the way. He needed my experience of working directly with church leadership, not always taking a no for an answer, and moving into new situations without much hesitation. As we continued our work, we also helped each other discover our own gifts in working with particular churches, but always with a global perspective.

TL: Over the past several years I have spent quite a lot of time traveling with Pakisa in many parts of Africa, and also in Latin America, Asia, North America, and Europe. Some years ago Pakisa was in a serious automobile accident, as a result of which today he walks slowly, using a cane. I've learned many things traveling with him—many things about time, for example, about urgency, about what one can see when one slows down. But I've also found it very instructive to watch Pakisa's interaction with others. It struck me that the way many people respond to him is such a good example of how our needs play an important role in freeing the gifts of others and allowing them to be expressed. So often I've noticed that airline attendants, security personnel, taxi drivers, and hotel or restaurant staff, who to me seem surly and indifferent, suddenly light up and become gracious, friendly, and helpful when they see Pakisa. His need—to have a suitcase carried, or a seat adjusted—is often a gift to others and an invitation to them to share their gifts. I've also learned that by associating myself with him, I, too, can often receive these gifts of special care, so sometimes I let him go first!

PT: The joy of self-discovery was another aspect that impressed me through this project. It was exciting to watch people's faces as they created a list of gifts and resources from their own churches. Many did not realize they had such rich churches. The joy came from recognizing that many things that are not traditionally considered gifts are actually gifts from God. My favorite aspect of our discussions on gift and gift sharing is about God's intention for the gifts he gives to his people. It is not hard for people to believe that all gifts come from God, and that he intends for those gifts to be shared. But when we talked about what happens when we keep our gifts to ourselves or when we hoard them, the discussion turned into a personal challenge. The Hebrew people with manna in the desert are a good example. Manna was given for free and people were only to collect what was needed for their families and for the day. When they tried to hoard, the manna rotted and spoiled. It was enlightening to watch people's eyes as they talked about rotten manna and what it meant for their own personal lives, as well as church life.

TL: There is nothing quite like watching people discover their gifts. I remember in one church we visited there was a young woman who had just graduated from Bible school. She was quiet and withdrawn. Her congregation had given her an assignment to work with teenagers. We asked her to play a leadership role in organizing a gathering of women with theological training. At first she was reluctant, saying that she wasn't capable of the work. But when we encouraged her to reconsider, she wrote, "If you still want me I am willing to help. At first I thought it is hard, but when I read your encouragement I said I will try my best to be myself." Her subsequent organizing work showed great creativity and competency. As she began to understand what she was capable of doing she became markedly more self-confident.

Perhaps It Was the Music

I think the first time I was struck by my great wealth was in Luanda, Angola, in 1999. It was a Sunday morning in November, and Pakisa and I had done a Gift Sharing workshop with one of the Angolan conferences the day before. We were visiting a number of congregations before our planned departure the following day.

Luanda is a city that has mushroomed from a sleepy tropical port in the 1960s to a sprawling African city of perhaps six million people today. Even now the part of the city that borders the ocean has a relaxed, peaceful, Mediterranean feel. That quality belies the violence of the city's history as the port of departure for over half of the slaves exported to the Americas, as well as of the more recent decades-long civil war in the interior, which claimed the lives of perhaps 1.5 million Angolans before ending in 2002. It is also the civil war that has created modern-day Luanda, as hundreds of thousands of people fled the destruction and insecurity of the war-torn interior for the shantytowns of the capital.

After driving through the dusty streets and alleyways of the capital for what seemed like a long time, we came to an area where we heard people singing. At first we could not see the source, as the cement block and tin, half-finished constructions of suburban Luanda all look much the same. When we got out of the car the volume of the music increased, and we noticed that it came from one of the buildings, slightly larger than the others, a short distance from where we stood. As we approached, I felt a strange power and beauty in that music, drawing me like a siren and producing in me a strong longing to be a part, to be surrounded and held by that sound.

Later, after my colleague had given a brief message, I came before the congregation to give words of greeting. The cement platform where I stood had a roof of tin which protected us from the sun or the rain, but the rest of the sanctuary was open to the sky; the walls of the church were shoulder height, and the floor was a dusty sand. Seated on the simple wooden benches was a brilliant, colorfully dressed assortment of children, youth, and young and old women, with just a few scattered men.

I recall struggling to decide what words I should offer them— this group about whom I knew so little and with whom I obviously had so little in common. I knew nothing of their theology, as they knew nothing of mine. I knew nothing of their joys, their sufferings, or their daily lives. Yet these were people who understood themselves to be part of a family of which I, too, considered myself a part. How could this be? What did it mean?

As I stood looking over all those beautifully different faces, I was overcome by one thought: What wealth! What incredible, lovely riches! And how terrible it would be not to be related to them! I felt weighted down with a kind of burden of gratitude, a sense that somehow, in ways I cannot understand, my connectedness to these people was both a fact and a wish, a statement of what is and what can be. It was like a clear, still voice that said, "This is the path . . . follow it!"

It must be said that other thoughts were in my mind as well. What a waste! What incalculable, unspeakable loss, if the gifts of this young child, of these old women, of this youth in this small congregation, in this forgotten corner of the world are lost to the church, lost to the world, lost to the intricate and unknown purpose for which God has given them. Lost for want of opportunity, lost due to war, hunger, disease, lost from being smothered by material things or misdirected desire, lost to boredom, to feelings of inferiority or superiority. What a waste.

I cannot account for the *gift* I received that morning, but it has not left me since. It is a gift of being able to see myself surrounded by riches, by wealth, by gifts. It is the sure knowledge that everything and everyone that **is** has been *given* by God, and as such has purpose, intent, potential. It is the understanding that there can be no more sacred duty, no more holy calling, than to release those gifts—in ourselves, in others, and in all of God's creation.

I don't remember what, in the end, my words of greeting were that morning in Luanda. I think I said something to the effect that I knew that I was related to them, and they to me, by the way they sang. And perhaps it was the music, their gift released into the air and reaching my ears, which brought with it this gift of sight.

Since that morning in Luanda we have traveled to many parts of Africa and to other continents as well. We have looked upon many congregations and church groups in every continent. And everywhere we have seen many differences: music— some familiar, some strange; languages—some that we understood, some that we didn't; faces—of different colors and dif-

> "Each person talked about how their church was sharing gifts. One was providing aid to refugee families. Another was giving food to needy families who were not members of the church. Another was operating a literacy program. Still another was working to repair a community water supply system. One church has started a food bank." *(Workshop participant, Costa Rica)*

ferent shapes; church buildings—large and small, new and old, proud and humble; youth, children, women, men; we've seen congregations that danced up and down the aisles and congregations that sat stoically still. We have seen and heard of many different kinds of gifts: conflict mediation, formation of women's leadership, transcultural missions, recycling trash, artisan work, marriage counseling, choreography, teaching instruments, praise music, interdenominational dialogue, Bible distribution, translation, cloth painting, clowns, brooms and gloves for clean-up, experience working against family violence, peace education, brick making—the list could go on and on. But nowhere have we seen a lack of gifts; never have we spotted an un-gifted person. This is the tie that binds us all—our givenness, and our invitation to participate in God's purpose through the sharing of our unimaginable diversity of gifts.

Why Gift Sharing?

When we began the first Global Gift Sharing workshop on a rainy day in Kinshasa in November 1999, I don't think we knew enough about the agenda of the proposal to be intimidated by the task. But the proposal arose out of a major shift within the churches and the world and was an effort to make a concrete response. Three aspects of this shift affect our subject. First, at the foundation is the realization that the vast majority of Christians—and for the first time the majority of members of our denominational family—are from Africa, Asia, and Latin America, while much of the control and power of church institutions remains in North America and Europe. It is estimated that by 2025 over two-thirds of the world's 2.6 billion Christians will be in Latin America, Asia, and Africa, and already today there are more Christians in each of these continents than there are in North America. In our own church family, close to 60 percent of the total membership is in Asia, Africa, and Latin America.

Second, in the world generally the economic disparity between rich and poor, and between North and South, continues to increase. For economic growth and almost all other indicators, the last 20 years have shown a very clear decline in progress toward greater equity as compared with the previous two decades. Today 20% of the world's population consumes 86% of the world's goods. The combined wealth of the world's 200 richest people hit $1 trillion in 1999; the combined income of the 582 million people living in the 43 least developed countries is $146 billion. Approximately 790 million people in the developing world are still chronically undernourished. Today, across the world, 1.3 billion people live on less than one dollar a day, three billion live on under two dollars a day, 1.3 billion have no access to clean water, three billion have no access to sanitation, two billion have no access to electricity. We've all heard many such statistics before.

Third, there are strong and stubbornly entrenched patterns in the relationships between churches in the South and in the North that contradict our biblical beliefs. Specifically, churches in Africa, Asia, and Latin America are understood as pri-

There can be no more sacred duty, no more holy calling, than to release those gifts—in ourselves, in others, and in all of God's creation.

marily "needy," while churches in Europe and North America are understood as "wealthy." Churches in the South are understood as "receiving," and churches in the North as "giving." Contrasting this way of viewing the world is the clear biblical message that all of God's creation is gifted, that all persons have a role to play and gifts to give to the whole body, the global church. At the same time, every part of the body—of the church, of creation—needs every other part.

Now there are varieties of gifts, but the same Spirit; and there are varieties of services, but the same Lord; and there are varieties of activities, but it is the same God who activates all of them in everyone. To each is given the manifestation of the Spirit for the common good . . . As it is, there are many members, yet one body. The eye cannot say to the hand, "I have no need of you," nor again the head to the feet, "I have no need of you." On the contrary, the members of the body that seem to be weaker are indispensable . . . (I Corinthians 12:4-7; 20-22).

Indeed, the interrelatedness of the varieties of gifts is a clear statement of God's redeeming plan for all. The sharing of gifts, by which the needs of all can be met and by which abundant life can take place, is God's purpose in the world.

In this light, the historical patterns which divide the global church into the "needy" and the "gifted" must be understood as one of the most damning heresies confronting Christianity today. It divides us in two and creates deep-rooted complexes of superiority and inferiority. It makes some of us feel that we don't need others at all, and it makes others of us feel that we can do nothing without the initiative of others. It causes some of us to think that sharing our gifts is an optional activity that gives us credit with God; it causes others to think that we have no gifts worthy of sharing. It gives great honor to certain gifts, such as material wealth and power and particular professions, while dishonoring and cheapening gifts such as hospitality, certain less lofty skills, and reliance on others. In these and many other ways, both subtle and overt, our false notion of gifts—and needs—divides and threatens the church.

The strength of these patterns could easily cause us to give up on a vision of churches that share gifts freely and globally, except for one thing. Everywhere we have visited the churches, in the East and the West, the North and the South, we have found many people who are energized and enthusiastic about the idea of having closer relationships with people who are different from them. However comfortable we may be in our local settings and our own traditions and habits, most of us feel drawn to differences—to the person who acts, speaks, dresses, eats, or worships in ways not like our own. Even when we disagree with the other and prefer our own way, still we often find these differences interesting and attracting. The possibility of a direct relationship with another congregation, or with other persons or groups whose circumstances are very different from ours, usually gives exuberant life to a congregation.

Where does this energy come from? What is its source? Is it simply a sense of boredom with the everyday, with the usual? Might there be something much more profound at play than that? Could it be that this desire for difference comes from a subconscious awareness of what God means for us to be—as individuals, as a church, as a people? Could it be a recognition that we can find fullness and completion in relationship with others who are different? Might it be an implicit acknowledgment that we learn more about God and God's purpose when we learn to know those who experience God differently than we do?

Why This Book?

This book has several intended purposes. First, it is an attempt to report on a specific experiment called Global Gift Sharing, which was undertaken by Mennonite World Conference beginning in the late 1990s. The intent was to help member conferences to become more aware of their own gifts and resources, and to use those gifts to build closer relationships among the various parts of the global church.

Second, because those of us who undertook this experiment learned so many things in the process—about the churches, about gifts, about sharing, about what God expects of the church, about obstacles to and opportunities for closer relationships—we wanted to share some of these discoveries with a wider audience. We hope this work can be used by churches and individuals of any denomination who are interested in similar goals.

Third, while most of our work has been at the level of national church conferences, everywhere we have gone people have expressed the need for gift discernment and sharing to take place at the congregational level. We hope this book will lend itself to use by congregations. We have included some materials in the Appendices (see page 113 and following) that may be helpful in organizing congregationally based gift sharing workshops.

Finally, we also want this book to be a thanks-giving to all the people we have met and worked with through the course of this program, people who have extended great hospitality, who have entrusted us with their creative thoughts and ideas, who gave the time and energy to make our efforts possible and successful. All of these participants have been great gift-givers and have taught us about gifts and sharing by their example.

2.
Many Gifts,
But the Same Spirit

What do you have that you did not receive?
And if you received it,
why do you boast as if it were not a gift?

(I Corinthians 4:7)

Gift Sharing. It seemed simple enough. Everybody knows about gifts. We have all given a gift at some time or another, and all of us can think of gifts we have received. Do we not all like to receive gifts, and do we not all find joy in giving gifts as well? Are not gifts a natural and important part of every culture, every society, even every religion?

Yes, but. One of the first issues we encountered when we visited churches and held workshops on Global Gift Sharing was different understandings of the word *gift*. At some of the Gift Sharing workshops, participants told us that as they were coming to the workshop others in their communities told them, "Please remember us when you start sharing." For these people the language of gifts and sharing was the language of material distribution.

We found essentially two sources of confusion regarding the term. First, because we were talking about gifts within the church, everyone assumed that we were interested only in *spiritual gifts*. We will look more closely at the concept of spiritual gifts in the following chapter, but let us note here that this is a term used by Paul in the New Testament. The apostle lists five, seven, eight, or nine different "spiritual gifts" in references in Romans, I Corinthians, and Ephesians. These variations might suggest that Paul is not making the case for a closed or fixed list of gifts that are "spiritual," as opposed to all others that are not. But for now let us simply say that when we speak of gifts and gift sharing we are interested in broad, inclusive definitions of these words. We want to consider the wide diversity of gifts which God has bestowed upon us as individuals, the church, and the world as a whole.

The second area of confusion surrounding the word *gift* is that many languages and cultures use several different words for gift. In Spanish, for example, there are the words *regalo* and *don*; in French *cadeau* and *don*; in English *present* and *gift*. Still other languages have distinct words for gifts that are given on different occasions—such as funeral gifts, wedding gifts, initiation gifts, and gifts given to God.

But beyond the issues of definition, we find that there are indeed, as Paul says in I Corinthians 12:4, a great "variety of gifts." Perhaps all of this variety can be grouped into two general categories. First, there is the material world, each element of which is or can be given or received as a gift. This would include the gifts of creation—the world, plants, minerals, animals—as well as all goods (including money) created by human beings from these material gifts given by the Creator.

Second, there are immaterial gifts. These can be special capacities or skills, which we also know as talents, or they can be one-time immaterial gifts, such as a visit or an act of service. Among these are the spiritual gifts that Paul mentions—preaching, teaching, prophecy, healing, and so on—but also artistic and musical capacities, and the ability to do almost any task with special skill, such as carpentry, food preparation, business activities, scientific investigation, farming, and more.

In this book we are concerned with both of these categories of gifts. The gifts needed by Christ's church, and the gifts which God has given us to use redemptively in the world, are as many and varied as the mind of God. Many gifts; the same spirit.

What Is a Gift?

It is not important to try to explain gifts in a definitive or comprehensive way. But from thinking about the above two general categories of gifts we can identify three characteristics that appear to be true of all different kinds of gifts. First, a gift is something that is *given*; it is something that moves from one person to another. Second, a gift is something given *voluntarily*. It cannot be forced or required. And third, a gift is something given voluntarily *without regard to compensation*. It is different from something sold or exchanged, where we expect equivalent value in return for what we give.

From these descriptive aspects of gifts, we can conclude that gifts are characterized by movement and a certain quality of freedom. There can be no such thing as a gift that isn't given, or more broadly, a gift that isn't used. In Exodus we find the story of the gift of manna, where God tells the Israelites to collect only enough for their daily use. When some of the people gather more than they need, intending to save it, the unused gift turns rotten and breeds worms. Gifts can't be stored, put in the bank, or held in abeyance. They must be given and used, or they lose their power, their goodness.

When we say that gifts are characterized by an aspect of freedom, we mean that a gift cannot be given under constraint. II Corinthians 9:7 states that "Each of you must give as you have made up your mind, not reluctantly or under compulsion, for God loves a cheerful giver." Often it is true that our giving is motivated by a sense of debt. We give because we feel that we owe someone, and by giving we can even the score. Alternatively we may give in order to create a debt for which we will later be repaid.

It is easy to see that this kind of giving is not about gifts. If we give to cancel or to create a debt, we are simply engaging in commerce or even bribery. Commerce has an important place in our lives, and we do not mean to say that it is a bad thing,

When Jesus himself gives to or receives from others, he generally does not attempt to achieve or maintain anonymity.

but it involves a different category of giving and receiving than gift sharing, and we should be careful not to confuse the two.

There is a freedom about a gift. It is *released* by the giver without strings attached. In this way a gift can be truly creative. It is able to interact as it will in the new environment of the person who receives it and thereby become something new. Sometimes we talk about gifts "going astray." This refers to a gift which was given for a specific purpose but was used in some other way by the receiver. But in a real sense gifts are meant to "go astray," and when we give with instructions about how the "gift" should be used, we are simply maintaining control in a way that qualifies our gift. To release a gift is to empower the receiver, to give the recipient something that she or he can incorporate and use in such a way that that person's own gifts—not the will or the intentions or the designs of the giver—can in turn be developed and released.

Are Gifts and Needs Opposites?

Earlier we introduced the question of gifts and needs, noting that the way we often divide the world into those who have needs and those who have gifts is highly destructive to all. The relationship between gifts and needs is one of the most difficult, and at the same time most critical, issues in our consideration of sharing the gifts God has given us. This is particularly true when we look at the global church, which includes, on the one hand, many people for whom the most basic needs of human survival have been met and, on the other, many who struggle daily to meet these same needs.

Often gifts and needs are seen as opposites, as the two poles of a continuum. In this view, a need is a request or a question and a gift is the answer. But as we have noted, this polarization leads to a kind of heresy that has been perpetuated for too long—that the world is made up of people with gifts and people with needs. If we believe as a matter of faith that all of creation is "gifted," that God has not created "ungifted" beings, then we must find another way to understand this relationship. As a matter of faith we believe that those who struggle for survival are no less gifted than those who have abundance. What then is the difference between them?

> Time, too, is a gift. We talk about being "given" time, about giving someone else time, about receiving time or having time. But it's a gift that is given and received—and kept and used—very differently in different cultures. A colleague once volunteered to talk with a group of American women about organizing a Gift Sharing workshop. She reported back to us: "They had many questions, about 'outcomes,' the practical difficulties of upkeep of any list of global gifts, and finally whether Americans have time to participate in such an effort. One representative said very bluntly, 'If you want to know what gifts I have to offer, make an appointment to call me at 11:30, and I'll talk with you for 15 minutes and tell you what they are.' I got a new insight into why it is difficult to get anything going in the U.S. for Global Gift Sharing—time is a gift most of us Americans don't think we have . . . . "
>
> It is as though, in some parts of our world, time has been fully transformed from gift into a commodity. When it is given, an equivalent return is expected. It is carefully parceled out into exact packages. It takes on value in itself without regard to its contents or how it is used.

We cannot in this book go into a detailed analysis of why there are the "poor" and why there are the "rich." Many others have done that analysis with great detail and, we must acknowledge, have come to differing conclusions. But whatever analysis we accept, we should be able to agree—as a church—that this state of affairs, this fundamental reality in our world, is not God's intention and is not a part of the vision of the kingdom toward which we are all called to work.

It should also be possible for us as a church to agree that some people have, for whatever reasons, been in a position to develop their gifts, while others, again for whatever reasons, have not. We came to understand this issue more clearly during a visit to the church in Nigeria. There as elsewhere we spent a lot of time meeting with groups of people from different dioceses of the church, encouraging them to think about the gifts they had and how they could share them with others. There seemed to be a good understanding of and enthusiasm for this concept, and the people acknowledged that they, individually and as a church, had many gifts.

But when we got to the stage of asking groups to list the gifts that they and their churches had, the response in Nigeria as in many other places, was consistently what seemed to us a list of *needs*. At first we attributed this to a problem of translation since we were often talking through interpreters. Alternatively we thought this might be due to historical conditioning; we were outsiders, agency people, and historically such visitors have always come asking, "What are your needs?"

Later we asked one of the bishops, "Why is it that when we ask about gifts, people speak to us of their needs? Are we not being understood?" The bishop's response was revealing: "Of course, we know that we have gifts and that we have many gifted people. But there are things that stand in the way of these gifts. That child over there is an orphan; her parents have both died of AIDS. She has no one to pay her school fees. How can her gifts be developed? And the choir that sang so beautifully for you, they have no uniforms, no resources for new instruments, no funds to pay for travel to other churches or for recording a cassette. How can they share their gift? We have many youth who already have university degrees, but the economy here is so bad that none of them can find work. How can they become supporting members of the church, and how can the church nurture their gifts?"

This exchange helped to lead us to a new understanding of gifts and needs, one that we should have seen before. Needs are not the opposite of gifts, but are much more intimately related. Why do the hungry need food and the sick need healing? So that the gifts God has endowed them with can be nurtured and can in turn be given. We could say that gifts "need" other gifts so that they can in turn be given. What we call a "need" then, can in fact be seen as a cry of invitation from a gift that is trapped and cannot be released or given.

If gifts cannot be given or are not given, they die or rot, and this is contrary to God's intention. God has poured out gifts to all creation, not for death but for "abundant life."

It is important that we be clear on this point, for within this understanding, those whom we consider "poor" and those whom we call "rich" are the same. Those whose gifts cannot be nurtured, and those whose gifts are hoarded or are otherwise not set free, face the same fundamental dilemma. Their gifts are kept from circulation, and as a result, in the language of Paul, the whole body suffers.

We have already referred to the well-known passage in I Corinthians, chapter 12, which is perhaps Paul's classic statement on gifts. But if we look closely, we see there are two other key themes in this chapter besides gifts. There is, first, the theme of the body. After introducing the idea of different gifts, Paul goes on to say:

> For just as the body is one and has many members, and all the members of the body, though many, are one body, so it is with Christ. . . . Indeed, the body does not consist of one member but of many (12, 14).

Thus Paul makes the case for the one and the many, the unity of the diverse gifts of the different members. But it is the third theme—*need*—that allows us to understand the whole illustration. It is *mutual need* that binds the many members, all with their unique gifts, into the one body.

> The eye cannot say to the hand, "I have no need of you," nor again the head to the feet, "I have no *need* of you." On the contrary, the members of the body that seem to be weaker are indispensable. . . (21-22).

The church would benefit by reflecting on that last sentence. In what way does our church believe, and actively demonstrate, that we need the weaker members of the body, that they are indispensable?

Need, then, can be seen as the vital link between gifts. Needs should not be understood as lacks, as simple absences. Needs are needed by gifts. They awaken gifts and function as a kind of gravity that draws gifts and uses them creatively to produce new gifts. Without needs—without use—there can be no gifts. And gifts in turn do not simply satisfy needs; rather they release gifts that can in turn seek out other needs.

In this way we could say that needs are in effect gifts to gifts, and gifts are gifts to needs. The relationship is always bi-directional; it allows the resources and potentials of both the giver and the receiver to become gifts, to be given. To deny need, whether our own or that of the other, is to deny the gifts God has given. Most importantly, it is the dynamic and mutual interplay of gifts and needs that make it possible for many members to be one body.

Sometimes when we want to offer our gifts we become so focused on need that we can lose sight of other fundamental motivations for giving. Trude Neufeld was already in her late seventies when I first met her at the church we began attending in Pennsylvania, where she was a founding member. She was a small woman who used a cane and was always attended by one or more of her middle-aged daughters. Trude had come to the U.S. as a refugee from Russia as a young child and had known all the privations and insecurities of refugees everywhere before she and her husband eventually built a successful business. Our

"What do you have that you did not receive? And if you received it, why do you boast as if it were not a gift?"

family became quite close to Mrs. Neufeld, and often she would bring us gifts of food, clothing, and money. With five young children we probably appeared to be quite needy.

For many years Trude spent much of her spare time sewing quilts which she gave for relief work. After she was retired and her husband had died, she continued making quilts, together with her daughters and others. One Sunday after church, shortly after I had returned from an administrative trip to Africa, I spoke with Mrs. Neufeld about the complexities of relief and development work, thinking all the time about some of the "waste" and "misuse" of relief supplies—such as the quilts she made—which I had observed. Finally she looked up at me with a smile, and said simply, "I am so grateful."

Only later did I realize that her words were actually a response to my comments; that she was saying it was out of gratitude for the gifts she had received that she in turn gave gifts. She had little interest in controlling the "good" her own gift might do. It was as though for her, need was simply an excuse to express gratitude.

Because We All Share in the One Loaf

Our topic is not simply gifts, but *gift sharing*. Why have we chosen this term; why not simply giving and receiving gifts?

Like the word gift, sharing is a word that has some ambiguity in many languages. In English, for example, it has nearly opposite or contradictory meanings. First, there is the sense that implies a division or separation—a property, a company, a sum of money, even food is divided into *shares*, separated, and distributed to different persons. This is the kind of sharing that the Prodigal Son had in mind when he said to his father, "give me the *share* of the property that will belong to me" (Luke 15:12). He was asking his father to divide up, to separate.

In contrast, sharing also has the meaning of participating together in a common task, event, or undertaking, or participating together in the use of some material thing. An example of sharing in this sense is when we speak of sharing responsibility, sharing leadership, or sharing a meal together. I Corinthians 10:17, which says in part "though we are many, yet we are one body, because we share in the one loaf," is another example of this kind of sharing.

Obviously it is in this second sense that we use the term *gift sharing*. It is true, as a participant in a workshop we held in Indonesia pointed out, that this whole effort is really concerned with *sharing*, as much as or more than with gifts. One could say that the phrase *gift sharing* is redundant; an act of sharing inevitably involves a gift.

In the process of translating our workshop materials into French, we came up against these contrasting meanings of "to share" in the French language. Originally we were translating "Gift Sharing" as *"Partage de dons."* Later it was drawn to our attention that this gave the wrong meaning. *"Partage de dons"* could be translated as something like "dividing up gifts." Our new title was completely different: *"Mise en commun des dons,"* which could be literally translated as "the placing/holding in common of gifts." These two translations demonstrate the two different meanings of "sharing." In particular, holding or placing in common conveys well the idea that sharing involves and requires a relationship.

Anonymous Gifts

Sharing is different than simply giving or receiving. It is possible to give a gift anonymously. Particularly in Western culture, anonymous giving is considered to be of the highest merit. Among the writings we have collected on gifts is the following list of the "Eight Degrees of Charity" by 12th century Spanish philosopher Rabbi Moses Ben Maimonides:

Degrees of Charity

• The first and lowest degree is to give, but with reluctance or regret. This is the gift of the hand, but not of the heart.
• The second is to give cheerfully, but not proportionately to the distress of the sufferer.
• The third is to give cheerfully and proportionately but not until solicited.
• The fourth is to give cheerfully, proportionately, and even unsolicited, but to put it in the poor man's hand, thereby exciting in him the painful emotion of shame.
• The fifth is to give charity in such a way that the distressed may receive the bounty and know their benefactor, without their being known to him . . . .
• The sixth, which rises still higher, is to know the objects of our bounty but remain unknown to them . . . .
• The seventh is still more meritorious, namely, to bestow charity in such a way that the benefactor may not know the relieved persons, nor they the names of their benefactors . . . .
• The eighth, and the most meritorious of all, is to anticipate charity by preventing poverty, namely to assist the reduced fellowman, either by a considerable gift or a sum of money, or by teaching him a trade, or by putting him in the way of

business, so that he may earn an honest livelihood and not be forced to the dreadful alternative of holding out his hand for charity.

Here a high value is placed on blind giving, where there is no connection between the giver and the receiver. This approach seems consistent with Jesus' words in the Sermon on the Mount, when he says:

> So whenever you give alms, do not sound a trumpet before you, as the hypocrites do in the synagogues and in the streets, so that they may be praised by others. Truly I tell you, they have received their reward. But when you give alms, do not let your left hand know what your right hand is doing, so that your alms may be done in secret; and your Father who sees in secret will reward you (Matthew 6:2-4).

In relation to this passage we should note, however, that the giving of alms was a religious duty for Jews. Jesus is not so much addressing the question of how we help sisters and brothers in need, but rather how we go about our religious duties. His concern here is not the relationship between the giver and the receiver, but the giver's response to religious obligations in general. In the verse immediately preceding the above passage Jesus makes this clear:

> Beware of practicing your piety before others in order to be seen by them. . . .

When Jesus himself gives to or receives from others, he generally does not attempt to achieve or maintain anonymity. To the contrary, the relationship between the giver and receiver is essential and emphasized. Jesus' gifts of healing are given directly, often through physical touch, and they are identified as coming from God. Likewise when Jesus receives a gift of anointing from a woman, he recognizes that she has done "a beautiful thing" to him and makes it clear that her gift will not be kept secret:

> Truly I tell you, wherever the gospel is proclaimed in the whole world, what she has done will be told in remembrance of her (Mark 14:9).

Sharing for Relationship

This is a good demonstration of the difference between giving/receiving and sharing. There is a place for giving and receiving, even for anonymous giving and receiving. But anonymous sharing is impossible. Sharing gifts is not an end in itself, nor is it primarily about making everyone more equal. Rather sharing is about building up the interrelatedness of the body, for our purposes, the church.

In a real sense gifts are meant to "go astray," and when we give with instructions about how the "gift" should be used, we are simply maintaining control in a way that qualifies our gift.

Many of the traditions surrounding funerals in Africa are being lost because of the great increase in the number of deaths due to HIV/AIDS. But traditionally a funeral was a time of community sharing. Everyone in the community comes to a funeral, and all members bring with them what they can, what they have. It can be money, food, livestock, clothes; it can be singing or a lengthy eulogy. All of these gifts have only one purpose. They are not to enrich the family of the deceased, but to build a stronger community. The gifts allow the family to take care of the needs of those who come to visit or sympathize, and as such the bonds among all members of the community are strengthened.

This interrelationship of the different parts of the body is important so that the body can do its work and fulfill its purpose. To say this in another way, we believe it is essential that the global church family develops a true sense of interrelatedness among the different parts of the family—parts that are separated by geography, history, culture, language, race, and many other factors. We need to become more real, more connected, to each other, not simply so we can have warm family feelings toward each other, but so we can empower our respective gifts to further God's purpose, God's vision for the world. It is through the *sharing* of gifts that relationships can be built, nurtured, and strengthened.

Indeed, we might consider whether it is not *only* through gift sharing that relationships can come about. Think about your own close relationships. Is not the sharing of gifts a crucial component in all of them? Can we imagine a relationship without gifts? In our relationships with our friends, our spouses, our parents, our children, our neighbors, the sharing of gifts is always central to them and to their growth and development.

It is *sharing*, then, that carries the relational freight when we think about gifts and how they are used. When gifts are shared (rather than simply "given") the world of the giver and the world of the receiver are made to overlap. Sharing implies that all of the parties involved become mixed up and are a part of, or belong to, what is being done.

For this reason it is often difficult to share material gifts. They are too mobile, too easily separated from the giver and from the relationship. Of course, material objects frequently do take on relational value. All of us have material things that have been vested with value because of their history, because of their provenance, because of who used them, because of the relationships they represent, rather than because of their *cost* or market value. I enjoy cooking and working in the kitchen, and a large measure of my joy in cooking comes from using utensils that have special meaning because of my relationships with the people who gave them to me.

We should point out that of all material gifts, money is the most mobile, the most detachable, and therefore the least relational. This is because money is always a substitute; in general it *represents* value rather than having any value itself. As a substitute for some material thing or things, for some service or potential service, it is disconnected and mercurial. Many of us have experienced giving or receiving money designated for a specific purpose. Because money is so versatile, both givers and receivers often are made to feel uncomfortable with restrictions and designations placed on its use.

On the other hand, it is for this same reason that most of the gifts that we have been able to identify among the churches throughout the world involve *human* resources, or institutional resources to which people are connected. These gifts share well because they cannot be easily separated from the receivers and givers; the worlds of both inevitably overlap and are shared when the gift is given and received. When you as a skilled woodworker or teacher or singer or cook give your skills as a gift, they cannot be separated from you, and so they are much more likely to involve a relationship.

To be clear, the emphasis on relationships should not be understood as a desire for homogenization, for becoming the same. The poet e.e. cummings once wrote, "False is alike: false teeth." The teeth God gives us are all different—some crooked, some straight, some larger, some smaller. As we have already noted, life and sameness don't go together. Sameness is sterile, dead.

We have found that all around the world, in very diverse cultures and societies and churches, on all of the continents, people long for direct connections with others. Congregations want to be in relationship with congregations that are different from them. There is a strong desire for sharing relationships. This is the motivating force for gift sharing.

> Relationships make possible the continuing existence of the universe. . . . The refusal to share is wrong. It is, in fact, an act of destruction because it does not serve to cement the bonding that is required to form community. Quite the contrary, it is perceived as an element that seeks to weaken and break such bonds (Laurenti Magesa, in *African Religion*).

3.
A Sharing God

Every generous act of giving,
with every perfect gift, is from above,
coming down from the Father of lights,
with whom there is no variation or shadow due to change.

(James 1:17)

Let us recall that the subject we are examining is how we as Christians are called to share gifts. In the previous chapter we saw that a gift is something that is voluntarily given from one person or entity to another without compensation. We also noted that sharing involves a process of giving and receiving which creates a relationship and an interconnection between giver and receiver. We have made some reference to the biblical basis for gift sharing, looking at various passages from the Bible. In this chapter we will consider more systematically and deliberately the principles that reflect the way that God shares gifts and how gift sharing is presented in Scripture.

Our models for gift sharing should be based on our understanding of the biblical accounts of how God has given and shared gifts. God's ways of sharing gifts are the primary examples we have to follow. In order to identify how God shares gifts we need to examine some of the gift stories available to us in the Bible. Genesis 1:27 sets the tone for understanding the stories that follow.

So God created humankind in his image, in the image of God he created them; male and female he created them.

Here the very image of God is shared with humankind. This demonstrates God's fundamental desire to be in relationship with humans through sharing gifts.

The Bible has many stories about giving, receiving, and sharing gifts, and we will look at some of these here. There are two gift stories, however, that are more important than all the others and on which our understanding of gift sharing is based.

The Creation Story

The first is the story of creation in Genesis. Here we learn of God's gift of the universe, including life itself. It is a gift given to all living things, not only to humans, and we can see that all the gifts of creation are related to each other.

We might begin by asking in what sense creation is a *gift*, an act of giving or sharing on the part of God. One could reason, to the contrary, that the creation of the universe, the world, and life itself simply represented an extension of God's domain, that the creation was the enhancement of what belonged to an omnipotent God, in the same way that the owner of a property might develop it by building a house on it or by improving the soil or by planting trees.

Genesis 1:28-30 is the very first occasion in the Bible where creation, specifically human creation, is addressed directly by the Creator. The language of these verses is clearly a language of giving, of gift:

God blessed them [humankind], and God said to them, "Be fruitful and multiply, and fill the earth and subdue it; and have dominion over the fish of the sea and over the birds of the air and over every living thing that moves upon the earth." God said, "See, I have given you every plant yielding seed that is upon the face of all the earth, and every tree with seed in its fruit; you shall have them for food. And to every beast of the earth, and to every bird of the air, and to everything that creeps on the earth, everything that has the breath of life, I have given every green plant for food."

It seems significant that in the biblical account, the whole history of interaction between God and humans begins with a declaration of gifts. In verse 28, God gives "dominion." This is followed by the verse that begins "See, I have *given* you . . . ," noting specific gifts to humans, while verse 30 notes God's gifts to other living creatures.

Manna is given to be used. When it is withdrawn into the realm of private ownership it becomes rotten.

What can we conclude from this creation account followed by God's initial "gifting" communication with creation? Let us consider several points.

First, *creation is the creative work of God.* This may sound like double-talk. But what we want to emphasize is that creation is *creative.* It is God's ingenuity. By beginning with the creation accounts the Christian Scripture makes the point that everything *comes forth* from God. All matter, all life, results from God's creative work. Creative work is different from just plain work, from simple production. In particular it is different because it contains within it an ingenuity that comes directly from the creator, that comes uniquely from the creator. Creation is not simply an assembly of parts, it involves an aspect, what we could call the "spirit," of the creator. Thus we can say that everything that is is "of God."

Historically Christians have taken the creation account to mean, among other things, that everything is owned by God, that God is the proprietor of all that is. Psalm 24 makes this point:

> The earth is the Lord's and all that is in it, the world, and those who live in it; for he has founded it on the seas, and established it on the rivers.

God's ownership is based on the fact that God is the creator of all.

We do not want in any way to call into question this aspect of ownership. But we suggest that our preoccupation with ownership may reflect a human cultural bias that obscures an equally important but different sense in which creation "belongs to" God. This is that all of creation contains God's spirit, God's creative genius. Creation is "of God," and God is in it.

Seen from this perspective of "belonging to," we can better understand humankind's dominion over "every living thing that moves upon the earth." The word "dominion" implies a very strong ownership—dominance, supremacy, ascendancy—even "absolute" ownership. It seems clear that God is giving to humans something more than a mere caretaker role. But this dominion is qualified by the fact that the earth and all that is in it, "every living thing that moves upon the earth," is of God and contains God's spirit within it, just as human beings themselves, as a part of creation, are of God. Thus nothing can ultimately be alienated from God, and human dominion is qualified by ongoing relatedness and interrelationship.

A second point that can be made based on the Genesis 1 passage is that *creation is always given.* Creation must of necessity be "offered up," released; it must go out from the creator. A creation is something that is born into a wider environment. In the case of the biblical creation, the mind of God, the purpose of God, the creativity of God is born into the universe.

In this sense creation is inevitably given (and received). Any work of art, for example, is given up when it is displayed. This doesn't necessarily mean that the artist no longer owns it, but a displayed work of art opens itself to diverse influences, uses, and responses beyond the artist herself or himself. Others can receive it and be changed by it, be moved by it, use it, and modify it, regardless of whether they physically own it.

In the same way, a work that is not released, that does not move out from its creator, can hardly be considered a creation. Creation cannot be contained or enclosed, nor can it carry a breath of life, the spirit of its creator, unless it moves out to touch others.

The third insight from the Genesis 1 account is that *creation is given to all,* not just to all human beings, which is in itself a revolutionary idea, but also to "everything that has the breath of life." In this we can see the "genesis" of the Biblical view of sharing. We might be tempted to understand verses 29 and 30 as supporting the more restrictive understanding of "share" that we noted in the previous chapter—to share as in to divide up, to separate, to designate; this part is given to human beings and this part to other life forms. But a more careful look shows that what is really at issue is a more complex interconnectedness which supports the "relationship" meaning of sharing.

This brings us to our final observation, that *creation is about interrelatedness.* Let us note the specific sequences of the Genesis 1 creation account. First, God created light and then separated it from darkness. Light is the first gift, and we know how closely related light is to all of life. The second gift is the sky, the atmosphere, followed by the seas and the land. The gifts of vegetation, creatures of the sea, the air, the land, and finally humans follow.

The great truth of both the most modern science and the most primitive religion is that everything is interrelated and interconnected. To say it differently, everything is in a "gift sharing" relationship with everything else. In God's creation there is no possibility of alienation or separation. Alienation, withdrawal from the sharing relationship, is certain death. Manna is given to be used. When it is withdrawn into the realm of private ownership it becomes rotten. God's purpose as expressed in creation is that gifts be shared.

The Jesus Story

The second great gift story of the Bible is of course the Jesus story, and in many ways it parallels the creation story. The initial verses of the gospel of John link Jesus to God, but also to creation:

> He was in the beginning with God. All things came into being through him, and without him not one thing came into being. What has come into being in him was life, and the life was the light of all people (John 1:2-4).

The language of "new creation" in II Corinthians 5:17 is similar:

> So if anyone is in Christ, there is a new creation: everything old has passed away; see, everything has become new!

John 3:16 shows that Jesus is to be understood as the creative work of God and that He is given as a gift to all creation:

> For God so loved the *world* that he gave his only Son, so that everyone who believes in him may not perish but may have eternal life.

Notice that both of these archetypal stories are stories of gift sharing, not simply gift giving. The fact that human life was created *in the image of God*, with God's own breath, shows that God didn't simply give the gift of life and the universe in a detached way, as though it were a machine that would do its own thing. Rather, God remained in relationship with creation; God's spirit was in the gift. The Jesus story is even more explicit on this point. Through Jesus, the "word became flesh, and dwelt among us." And the whole story of God's interaction with people is a story of God's desire to stay in relationship, despite the human tendency toward alienation, expropriation, and separation.

The biblical foundation of gift sharing rests on these stories, which together are the archetype for gift sharing. On the one

Gifts for Jesus

(Luke 7:37-48)

And a woman in the city, who was a sinner, having learned that he was eating in the Pharisee's house, brought an alabaster jar of ointment. She stood behind him at his feet, weeping, and began to bathe his feet with her tears and dry them with her hair. Then she continued kissing his feet and anointing them with the ointment. Now when the Pharisee who had invited him saw it, he said to himself, "If this man were a prophet, he would have known who and what kind of woman this is who is touching him— that she is a sinner."

Jesus spoke up and said to him, "Simon, I have something to say to you." "Teacher," he replied, "Speak." "A certain creditor had two debtors; one owed five hundred denarii, and the other fifty. When they could not pay, he canceled the debts for both of them. Now which of them will love him more?"

Simon answered, "I suppose the one for whom he canceled the greater debt." And Jesus said to him, "You have judged rightly."

Then turning toward the woman, he said to Simon, "Do you see this woman? I entered your house; you gave me no water for my feet, but she has bathed my feet with her tears and dried them with her hair. You gave me no kiss, but from the time I came in she has not stopped kissing my feet. You did not anoint my head with oil, but she has anointed my feet with ointment. Therefore, I tell you, her sins, which were many,

> have been forgiven; hence she has shown great love.
> But the one to whom little is forgiven, loves little."
> Then he said to her, "Your sins are forgiven."

hand, God's spirit remains in the creative work of creation. This doesn't mean that God's gifts have strings attached; rather it means simply that God is a part of the material and other gifts we receive, and in receiving them we enter into a relationship with God. On the other hand, it also means that what God has given us is not ours to possess or to alienate but to share. God did not create a divided-up, parceled-out world, a world of separated, independent entities. Instead, God invites us to use our diverse gifts to build and reinforce the oneness of creation, the body of Christ.

These two key stories—of creation and of Jesus—powerfully demonstrate what we think are the most important biblical principles about gifts: 1) that all gifts come from God, 2) that it is God's purpose that gifts be shared, 3) that all people are equitably gifted by God, and 4) that the ultimate objective of biblical gift sharing is the redemption of creation. Let us consider briefly each of these principles.

All Gifts Come from God

We have seen that God is the original source of everything. This is the starting point of our understanding of gifts. Not only is this a key understanding of our faith, it is also the point of departure for virtually all other faiths. The basis of this belief for Christians is that our God is the God of all creation. The creation stories in Genesis show how God created everything; thus every thing that is comes from and belongs to God.

The Jesus story also unquestionably emphasizes God as the source of this gift. When the Bible speaks of Christ as God's son, it is a way of saying from where this gift has come. We all know that children come from their parents; by saying that Jesus is the son of God, the Bible affirms that Jesus is a gift from God to us.

God Intends That Gifts Be Shared

As we have noted, God's model for gifts is sharing rather than giving. In many ways this principle seems obvious. What other purpose could there be for gifts than sharing them? Can we imagine a great preacher who does not preach to a congregation? Or a person with a beautiful voice who does not sing for others? Can we imagine a tree or plant that refuses to

Jesus is to be understood as the creative work of God and that He is given as a gift to all creation: "For God so loved the world that he gave his only Son, so that everyone who believes in him may not perish but may have eternal life."

give oxygen and fruits to birds and animals? Imagine if the earth refused to give nutrients to plants. Imagine if a mother refused to give milk and love to a child. Imagine if a person with food refused to feed a person who was hungry. If a gift is not used, not given, not shared, none of us can survive, and God's universe cannot work.

In I Timothy 4:14 and 16, Paul writes to his young companion:

> Do not neglect the gift that is in you, which was given to you through prophecy with the laying on of hands by the council of elders. Put these things into practice, devote yourself to them . . . for in doing this you will save both yourself and your hearers.

Sharing the gifts we have is not just a nice thing to do, it is the reason we have been given gifts by God, and as Paul notes, putting our gifts into practice—sharing them—will save ourselves and others.

All People Are Equitably Gifted by God

To maintain that all people are equitably gifted by God means that God has given gifts according to each person's need as well as the needs of the whole. This allows—this requires—the participation of each person and each part of creation.

The word "equitable" suggests fairness and justice. While the word "equal" implies sameness, equitable implies *difference*—two or more *different* things that are both of value. This means that no one gift should be considered more valuable or more "spiritual" than another. God's creativity is in each, and if this is so, who can say that any person is more important or more gifted than any other person?

The Talents

(Matthew 25:14-29)

For it is as if a man, going on a journey, summoned his slaves and entrusted his property to them; to one he gave five talents, to another two, to another one, to each according to his ability. Then he went away.

The one who had received the five talents went off at once and traded with them, and made five more talents. In the same way, the one who had the two talents made two more talents. But the one who had received the one talent went off and dug a hole in the ground and hid his master's money.

After a long time the master of those slaves came and settled accounts with them. Then the one who had received the five talents came forward, bringing five more talents, saying, "Master, you handed over to me five talents; see, I have made five more talents." His master said to him, "Well done, good and trustworthy slave; you have been trustworthy in a few things, I will put you in charge of many things; enter into the joy of your master."

And the one with the two talents also came forward saying, "Master, you handed over to me two talents; see, I have made two more talents." His master said to him, "Well done, good and trustworthy slave; you have been trustworthy in a few things, I will put you in charge of many things; enter into the joy of your master."

Then the one who had received the one talent also came forward, saying, "Master, I knew that you were a harsh man, reaping where you did not sow, and gathering where you did not scatter seed; so I was afraid, and I went and hid your talent in the ground. Here you have what is yours."

But his master replied, "You wicked and lazy slave! You knew, did you, that I reap where I did not sew, and gather where I did not scatter? Then you ought to have invested my money with the bankers, and on my return I would have received what was my own with interest. So take the talent from him, and give it to the one with the ten talents. For to all those who have, more will be given, and they will have an abundance; but from those who have nothing, even what they have will be taken away."

Let us look at the story of Moses in Exodus 4. God has told Moses to go to the leaders of Israel in captivity in Egypt and tell them what God has prepared for them. Moses replies, "But suppose they do not believe me or listen to me?" In response God gives Moses additional gifts, different signs to convince the elders of Israel (4:2-9). But Moses still lacks confidence in his gifts and says, "I have never been eloquent . . . I am slow of speech and slow of tongue." So God provides Moses with Aaron who has the gift of fluent speech (4:14-15). Aaron's gift is not the same as Moses's, but it is just as important to the fulfillment of God's plan.

It is the same in other parts of creation. A tree cannot fly, but it creates and gives the gift of oxygen which allows birds to fly. The ground cannot grow into a flower, but unless it gives its gifts to the seed, the flower cannot grow. Thus we can say that all parts of creation and all people are equitably gifted, that the gifts of all are needed, that God's universe is a unity of differences.

The Purpose of Gift Sharing Is Abundant Life

Why does God wish us to share our gifts? In a sense the answer is simple. God's purpose for sharing gifts is the fulfillment or redemption of all creation through abundant life. This is clear in Paul's words to Timothy: "For in doing this you will save both yourselves and your hearers." But what is the nature of this abundant life?

First, the sharing of gifts creates the oneness of the church, and without the sharing of our gifts there can be no oneness. In I Corinthians 12 Paul talks about oneness and gifts. Beginning in verse 4 of chapter 12, Paul says that there are many varieties of gifts, but only one source. In verse 6 he claims that "it is the same God who activates all of them in everyone." Verse 7 stresses that gifts are given to each person "for the common good"; not for the lifting up of the gifted person, not for that person's comfort or glory, but for the good of all.

Paul then uses the metaphor of the physical body to show how the sharing of gifts among members is essential. He stresses the importance of diversity and the value of members who are considered "inferior." And finally, in verses 27-30, Paul states that God has given individual gifts for the good of the body as a whole.

Acts 4:32-37 demonstrates the living out of this philosophy in practical terms. The author tells how the members of the church in Jerusalem "were of one heart and soul" and shared all of their possessions.

The second statement we can make about the nature of the abundant life brought by the sharing of gifts is that this oneness of the church is intended to further God's plan for an interconnected, interrelated universe of justice and peace. Again, this comes about through the sharing of gifts. We can see this clearly in the laws of the year of Jubilee, set out in Leviticus 25. Here God makes provision for gifts which have been accumulated over time, which had been taken out of circulation, to be shared in order that those who have needs—slaves, widows, orphans, the poor, the disenfranchised—can be put back on an equitable

The Widow and Abundance
(I Kings 17:10-16)

When he came to the gate of the town, a widow was there gathering sticks; he called to her and said, "Bring me a little water in a vessel, so that I may drink." As she was going to bring it, he called to her and said, "Bring me a morsel of bread in your hand."

But she said, "As the Lord your God lives, I have nothing baked, only a handful of meal in a jar, and a little oil in a jug; I am now gathering a couple of sticks, so that I may go home and prepare it for myself and my son, that we may eat it, and die."

Elijah said to her, "Do not be afraid; go and do as you have said; but first make me a little cake of it and bring it to me, and afterwards make something for yourself and your son. For thus says the Lord the God of Israel: The jar of meal will not be emptied and the jug of oil will not fail until the day that the Lord sends rain on the earth."

She went and did as Elijah said, so that she as well as he and her household ate for many days. The jar of meal was not emptied, neither did the jug of oil fail, according to the word of the Lord that he spoke by Elijah.

footing with others. It is one of the main themes of the prophets that hoarding and accumulating gifts while others are in need is sin against God and God's purpose.

If we truly believe that all gifts come from God, and if we believe that it is God's plan that all gifts be shared with all creation, then it becomes clear that sharing gifts is not primarily a matter of being nice and doing good works. It is essential to our being faithful to God. It is just. Peace comes when we joyfully turn away from the desire to hold gifts for ourselves and release them to the good of all.

A Note About Spiritual Gifts

We return now to the question of spiritual gifts which we introduced in the previous chapter. The term "spiritual gift" in the Bible is used almost uniquely by Paul. If we study Paul's use of the word "spiritual" we note that in general it seems to be contrasted to "material," as in Romans 15:27:

> . . . for if the Gentiles have come to share in their spiritual blessings, they ought also to be of service to them in material things.

and again in I Corinthians 9:11:

> If we have sown spiritual good among you, is it too much if we reap your material benefits?

We should be clear that Paul is not depreciating material gifts. Indeed, in both of these passages the writer's point is that material and spiritual gifts belong together and complement each other; both are needed.

One warm Sunday morning in a small Methodist church in Durban, South Africa, I [Tim] found my mind wandering during what seemed to me an uninspired sermon. But then I heard the pastor say something which caught my attention. I don't remember the context or the topic of his sermon, but his words were, "When things are used they are material to us. If we give them to others they become spiritual to us and material to others." Since then I have reflected much on this statement, and it seems so obviously true that I don't know why I never thought of it myself. I like the idea that gifts can be both spiritual and material at the same time, and that they can change from one state to the other, or be spiritual for one person while being material for another.

At no point in the Bible does Paul, or any other writer, present a definitive list of gifts that are specifically labeled "spiri-

> "This church has been studying the theme of gifts for several weeks, trying to discover what gifts they have. There are many brothers and sisters who are not sure of their gifts, and they have had lively and fruitful discussions. It is important to note that the church is used to thinking only of spiritual gifts, and thus the brothers and sisters have said that to think of talents and skills as gifts that can be shared is something new for them.
>
> "When we came to this workshop on gift sharing we didn't know what to expect. We only thought about spiritual gifts. Many of us wanted to know what our own gifts are. Others wanted to know how to develop or use their gifts. We have learned that we have the responsibility to share the gifts that God has given us. It is not only spiritual gifts that can be used to serve God and other people. Now I feel that we have a clear idea of what gifts are and a Christ-centered model of how to use gifts." *(Workshop participants, Costa Rica)*

tual." In Romans 6-8 he lists seven different gifts—prophecy, ministry, teaching, exhortation, giving, leadership, and compassion; in I Corinthians 12 there are two lists, one in verses 8-10 and the other in verse 28. Another list is seen in Ephesians 4:11. All of these lists are different.

It seems clear from these passages that it is not Paul's purpose to establish a clear category of what is and what is not a spiritual gift. Rather, in each case the writer is concerned with unity in the church. The variety of gifts, services, and activities are all activated by the same God. The real test of gifts for Paul is whether they are used for the common good: "To each is given the manifestation of the Spirit for the common good" (I Corinthians 12:7).

Paul, then, reaffirms the fundamental themes discussed above, that all gifts come from God, and that all have gifts.

> But each has a particular gift from God, one having one kind and another a different kind (I Corinthians 7:7).

All of these gifts of God are "spiritual," since they originate with the Spirit. The critical question lies in whether or how gifts are shared. If we all have gifts, and if these gifts come from God and have a God-given purpose, then it is especially important that none of these gifts be wasted or misused. For this reason, a primary task of the church—both at a local congregational level, as well as at a global level—is to discern, lift-up, nurture, and release the gifts of all of its members.

Conclusion

Our talking about the biblical basis for sharing gifts with people in churches around the world has generated many interesting theological discussions. In Ghana, a participant noted that sometimes there are gifts that we want to keep and don't want to pass on. There was a lively discussion about whether this was sometimes the case with the Gospel. We receive it as a gift, it is something valuable, and we make it our own. Sometimes we may feel it is too valuable to be shared, or that it should only be shared with certain conditions attached.

In another workshop the question was asked whether, if we believe that all gifts come from God, there can be bad gifts. Or is it simply a matter of gifts being misused? It was agreed that there are some gifts that we should not accept because of what they may do to us or require of us.

Usually the gift sharing workshops were opened with meditations given by participants. We were always enriched by new insights coming from these presentations. A Congolese pastor emphasized that the diversity of our gifts should contribute to the material and spiritual development of the church. He noted that for many years the Congo church has shared its gift of music on many occasions with other parts of the church. He further noted that, "In music, the notes of the scale are all needed to make an agreeable sound—one note on its own is not interesting. In the church we have many gifts, but often they are disorganized. Our different gifts are like different notes of music; they need to be arranged and put together in a harmonious way. The time has come for our community to put all our gifts together for the good of all."

The most important aspect of Global Gift Sharing has been to allow people to look upon their capacities as valuable gifts. In Asia we met a dentist who had always dreamed of serving God in another country but regretted that she did not have any gifts to share. Though she was active in her church, the idea that her skill in dentistry was a gift that could be shared had never occurred to her. Through our discussions she realized

It seems significant that in the biblical account, the whole history of interaction between God and humans begins with a declaration of gifts.

that her skills in dentistry were a gift from God, and she asked us to help find a way for her to share her gift with the global church.

In each church workshop we spent some time talking about the ways that sharing is understood in the cultures and societies of the participants. Often the group concluded that, in the end, the cultural principles of how gifts are shared often differ very little from the biblical principles. This in turn led to some interesting questions in some of the groups. "Why is it," one young Congolese man asked, "that we will automatically bring generous gifts to a neighbor's wedding or funeral, but the offerings in our churches aren't enough to support our pastor, let alone reach out to others?"

Culture can sometimes be an impediment to sharing gifts. In one African setting we found that participants in the workshop were reluctant to single out any one person's gift. As a result they made a long list of all of the pastors in the church, saying that all of them were gifted preachers. In a similar vein, participants in a workshop in Japan pointed out that sharing gifts was not easy in the Japanese culture, which tends to repress diversity. In this context it would be considered immodest for individuals to mention their own gifts. They concluded that an emphasis on community could provide a safe context in which to highlight each others' gifts.

We have attempted to understand what the Bible tells us about the use of gifts. Our task is, in our own small ways, to follow the model of God's creation, to join in God's intention that the gifts we have been given be used for the good of all. We know that we have all been given gifts by God, for we have been created by God, in God's image, which means that we have been created with the possibility of being creative ourselves. We all have gifts, and we all have the possibility of letting our gifts flow and be of service to others. Through such sharing of gifts the body of Christ, the church, can move toward wholeness.

4.
Sharing Gifts
in the Global Family

. . . their abundant joy and their extreme poverty
have overflowed in a wealth of generosity on their part. . . .
they voluntarily gave according to their means,
and even beyond their means,
begging us earnestly for the privilege
of sharing in this ministry . . . .

(II Corinthians 8:2-4)

What do we mean by *"family"*? How do families differ from culture to culture, and even from one family to the next within the same culture? What about the negative experiences that some people associate with family? How is it helpful to talk about our church in different parts of the world as a "global family"?

"Family," like the apostle Paul's term "body," is a rich metaphor for the church. Because so many of us understand from our own experience the ties of affection, mutual responsibility, and common values that ideally exist within families in our different societies and cultures, we can appreciate some of the implications of using family as a model for the global

---

church. Since we all come from particular families, a part of the value of the metaphor is also recognizing the great diversity of what "family" can look like. Our individual experiences also make us acutely aware of how hard it is to make the family a place of inclusion where different gifts can be nurtured and encouraged, while maintaining cohesion and common values.

French sociologist Pierre Bourdieu notes that family

> . . . is a world in which the ordinary laws of the economy are suspended, a place of trusting and giving—as opposed to the market and its exchanges of equivalent values—or, to use Aristotle's term, *philia*, a word that is often translated as "friendship" but which in fact designates the refusal to calculate; a place where interest, in the narrow sense of the pursuit of equivalence in exchanges, is suspended.

There are many different levels of family. One of the most general dictionary definitions of family has to do with common ancestry. Thus at the broadest level, God's family includes all of creation since we recognize God as the Creator of all. In the last chapter we noted that God's creation is a web of interrelationship and that enhancing this relatedness is God's purpose for the world. Thus in a sense we are all part of a family under God, the Creator of all. It is not by accident that the Apostle Paul combines concepts of creation with those of family when he writes of the vision of God's ultimate purpose in the book of Romans:

> I consider that the sufferings of this present time are not worth comparing with the glory about to be revealed to us. For the creation waits with eager longing for the revealing of the children of God; for the creation was subjected to futility, not of its own will but by the will of the one who

We should not abandon the concept of family simply because of its shortcomings.

subjected it, in hope that the creation itself will be set free from its bondage to decay and will obtain the freedom of the glory of the children of God. We know that the whole creation has been groaning in labor pains until now; and not only the creation, but we ourselves, who have the first fruits of the Spirit, groan inwardly while we wait for adoption, the redemption of our bodies (Romans 8:18-23).

"Children of God," childbirth, "adoption"; this is family language.

A second level of family is what we call the "family of faith," which refers to those who share common beliefs in and about God, a common religion. We also refer to our denominational families, which indicate groups which share specific traditions and convictions within the larger Christian family. This is at times broken down further into specific church families and ultimately congregational families.

Our theme of gift sharing in the global family refers primarily to our denominational family, but we should keep in mind that as a denomination we are simply a branch in a larger family, which ultimately includes all of God's creation. For it is in this larger arena that our purpose as a denomination, as a church, is found.

The Purpose of the Global Family

In its most nuclear sense the family is where children are born, raised, and nurtured. To what purpose? Not to create a permanent cocoon of protection. Not to enhance the power and wealth of the nuclear family unit. Not to create an empire with secure borders, but for a different kind of expansion—for *abundant life.* We rejoice when we see our children using their gifts and receiving gifts from others, when we see them moving out on their own, becoming friends with and being recognized by others.

It is no accident that God's repeated command to "every living creature that moves" is to "be fruitful and multiply, and fill the earth." This command is entrusted to the family. In the story of Noah, after the flood God says to Noah:

> "Go out of the ark, you and your wife, and your sons and your sons' wives with you. Bring out with you every living thing that is with you of all flesh—birds and animals and every creeping thing that creeps on the earth—so that they may abound on the earth, and be fruitful and multiply on the earth" (Genesis 8:16-17).

Note that what comes out of the ark are basic family units—
"you and your wife," "your sons and your sons' wives," and the
birds and animals of which there were "two of every kind,
. . . male and female."

Often when we think of families we are concerned with
boundaries, with who is in and who is out, who is part of the
family and who is not. A family, or a congregation or a
church, can easily turn into a fortress caught up in protect-
ing those who are in from those who are out. This leads to
isolation rather than to relationship and often causes us to
think that we as a family have no need for the larger body.

It is important, and for most of us necessary, to have families in the narrow sense, with defined boundaries and limits,
grouping people on the basis of certain commonalities. But
the purpose of family is not to protect and shield the common ground, the common tradition, the common blood, from
people who are outside. To the contrary, a family is to nurture its members and then release them, and to enrich them
through contact and relationships with "the outside." Our
individual gifts contain God's spirit, and they have been
given to us so that they can be developed and used for the
common good.

God's invitation to life—and to human beings in a special
way—to "be fruitful and multiply" is not simply a command
to procreate or to take possession. More fundamentally it is
an urging, an encouragement to "go forth," to take one's gifts
and use them to build relationships in and with God's world.
It should be clear that this is not an invading, conquering
"going forth"; it is not an imperial, colonial expansion which
aims to make others more like ourselves. It is a *going forth*
that gives itself, that encounters other gifts and enters into
sharing relationships with others.

It is relevant to note that in the Bible, as in the vast majority of known religions, cultures, and societies on earth, incest is forbidden. This is not because incest is inherently a morally reprehensible act, but because, as the French writer René Girard notes, incest plays "an extreme role in the destruction of differences." It combines like with like. It defeats the purpose of God's plan for the interrelationship of diverse gifts. And this interrelationship is the purpose that has been entrusted to our global family.

Different Kinds of Families

If the family is the place where gifts of individuals are nurtured and prepared for sharing with others outside the family, then we should celebrate the fact that there are many different kinds of families—families with different make-ups, different ways of providing nurture. The idea that a family must be a mother, father, and children, for example, has no particular universal validity and no exclusive biblical basis. In biblical times "family" could be understood much more broadly, at times including all relatives by blood and marriage, but also servants, employees, and even livestock.

In virtually all parts of the world today many families have only one parent. Many families are made up of people who have no blood relationships but are linked solely through adoption and marriage. It is common for families to include extended family members, including nephews and nieces, grandparents, and younger siblings of the mother or father. Families can also be constructed of couples living without children or of single persons who find ways to deliberately nurture the gifts of others. Increasingly today with the advent of HIV/AIDS, there are families which include unrelated AIDS orphans and other

When I [Pakisa] was a child in Congo I was close to my older brother; it was he who often took care of me when my parents were out working in the fields. Once as a young man I was staying with him, his wife, and their four year old daughter Annie. At one point Annie crawled up on my lap and asked, "Can I come and live with you, Pakisa?" "You'll have to ask your mother and father," I told her. She did so, and later her parents told me, "You've been like a son to us since we were married, so if you want to take her, she can go with you." So Annie came to live with me for three years. Later after I was married and had finished my schooling we lived in Kikwit, and Annie came to stay with us. We formally adopted her after her father died in 1993.

families in which the deaths of parents have led to older children acting as parents to their younger siblings. All of this diversity can be seen positively, as gifts God has given us.

At the same time as we embrace the metaphor of family as the context for global gift sharing, we need to keep in mind that for many persons from both traditional and non-traditional families, family has not been a nurturing experience. Recently I [Tim] heard from a close friend with whom I had been out of touch for nearly 30 years. Reflecting on her conservative Christian community and family background, she wrote, "Are you strongly involved in the church? I don't want you to think I have anything against the church now; I'm very glad for the good parts of how I was raised. It was just hard to sort them out from all the ugliness when I was young. What I never told you is that I was verbally, physically, and sexually abused as a young child. None of it was extreme, but it was enough to damage me emotionally and cause me to choose the wrong people over and over in the process of resolving things inside. I'm a very spiritual person now; I just had to find my own spirituality."

The task of being family is a difficult one, and many things can go wrong in all different kinds of families. A parent may abandon his or her family, children and wives are often mistreated and abused, and external conditions such as unemployment, poverty, and ill health can have a damaging impact on families.

Nevertheless, the need for primary units where nurture takes place is universal, and we should not abandon the concept of family simply because of its shortcomings.

Thus when we use the term "family" in the context of the church, whether at a congregational or global level, we summon a whole array of characteristics such as inclusion, nurture, common values, outreach, all of which can be summed up in the invitation to abundant life.

The Abundant Life

The gospel of John quotes Jesus speaking to the Pharisees: "I came that they may have life, and have it abundantly" (John 10:10). This is a statement of purpose-Jesus's mission statement. And it is the same as God's purpose in creation; it is the same as God's promise and vision throughout the biblical story.

What exactly is this abundant life? The dictionary defines abundance as "more than sufficient," "overflowing fullness." We are reminded of the 23rd Psalm—"my cup overflows." It is important that we understand that God's intention for life is abundance, overflowing fullness. It is not just to get by. God's creation is such that living organisms receive far more energy than they need simply to survive. It is said that the sun delivers

When I truly share my gifts I am not losing anything.

enough energy to the earth in 40 minutes to supply all of the world's energy needs for a year. Life forms on earth use a small portion of that energy to produce extravagantly, abundantly. Different organisms *need* each other, need to be related to each other. And if the interrelationships between organisms are working properly, each organism exhibits an "overflowing full-ness" by producing far more than it needs to survive. Shortage (hunger, poverty, lack) is not a part of God's creation or plan.

Tanzanian theologian Laurenti Magesa writes that the ethical demands of traditional African religion can be summed up in one word—hospitality, or "open hearted sharing." "The purpose of hospitality," Magesa continues, "is to enhance life in all its dimensions." Here again the connection between sharing and abundant living is perfectly clear. "Open hearted sharing" does not deplete our resources; it does not make us poorer. Like the child who offered to share his bread and fish (John 6), the result of sharing is abundance.

This is opposite of our normal way of thinking about giving. Do we not ask ourselves "what we can afford" to give? Indeed, do not our churches and church agencies invite us to give "what we can afford," or "according to our means"? That question assumes that giving is loss, subtraction, that it takes away from what we have. Perhaps here again we need to emphasize the distinction between giving and sharing. Sharing creates abundance because there is no alienation involved. When I truly share my gifts I am not losing anything; instead I am extending myself, my gifts, toward another person, and in the process I am becoming a part of empowering that person's own gifts.

In II Corinthians 8, Paul makes a remarkable statement. Commenting to the church in Corinth about the Macedonian churches' response to the needs of believers in Jerusalem, he says "for during a severe ordeal of affliction, their abundant joy and their extreme poverty have overflowed in a wealth of generosity on their part." We might wish to rearrange this verse to say "for despite their extreme poverty and a severe ordeal of affliction, their abundant joy has overflowed in a wealth of generosity on their part." But no, it is the joy *and* extreme poverty that overflow in sharing. Is this an editor's error? Or is it possible that the Macedonians understood through their abundant joy that their poverty left them with few options other than to share. Paul says in verse 4 that they begged for "the privilege of sharing." Perhaps the Macedonian churches perceived, because of their poverty, the great value of being in relationship, in communion with others.

This is an example of the abundant life that God promises. When Jesus in the book of John speaks of having life abundantly, he refers to eternal life, to becoming a part of God's purpose and God's life through sharing. Sharing the abundant gifts we have received, allowing our cups to overflow, is the way we can join in God's purpose.

5.

Obstacles to Sharing Gifts

*How does God's love abide
in anyone who has the world's goods
and sees a brother or sister in need
and yet refuses help?
Little children, let us love, not in word or speech,
but in truth and action.*

(I John 3:17-18)

We have now made our way through a great deal of biblical reflection, theory, and illustrations about the gifts God has given us, and about the many benefits of sharing these gifts in the global church. So why, if all this is true, is it so difficult for so many of us to share? And especially if sharing is so integral to God's purpose for the world, why is it so difficult for Christians to share within the global church family? Can we really call ourselves a family at all when the differences between us are so great and so divisive? Are we really serious when we talk about our "brothers and sisters in Christ"? If we look at the needs and gifts we have collectively which go unmet on the one hand or unused on the other, doesn't the phrase "brothers and sisters in Christ" amount to profanity, to taking the name of the Lord in vain?

In this chapter we want to reflect on what it is that stands in the way of our sharing gifts. We should acknowledge from the start that this is a difficult thing to really talk about as a family. Many are wary of the subject, and we listen for key words or phrases that might allow us to classify the writer or speaker as either for us or against us. We fear being cast as guilty; we fear being seen as victims. We fear being preached to or patronized or misunderstood. We fear we will be judged by people who don't really know us, who don't know the problems and realities we face and the needs we have.

As writers we have our own views on these issues—why the world works the way it does, why life is so much more difficult for some than for others, and why there are such gulfs between us as sisters and brothers. But to mount a strong argument, laying out our views on why real sharing often does not happen in the family, would contradict one of the primary points of this book. We believe that in the worldwide family we all need each other, or stated more positively, that we all have valuable gifts for each other. Our role is to help make it more possible for churches to be in relationship with each other so that sharing and understanding can take place. Sisters and brothers can only come to know each other as a result of direct relationships with each other. Relationships cannot be done by proxy. Problems do not disappear when there is a relationship, but we do believe that all problems can be borne when they are shared.

At the same time, it would be wrong not to talk about these obstacles, because they are so destructive to the family. But it should be clear that we raise them first and foremost because we are convinced that it is possible—and necessary—to overcome them together.

Communication

If it is true that sharing happens in the context of relationship, then communication becomes an overriding prerequisite for gift sharing. A sister or brother with whom we cannot communicate is a member of the family with whom we cannot have a relationship.

In the world today, communication with each other is more possible than ever before. The Internet has made electronic communication a reality between distant locations which are in some cases inaccessible even to postal communications. Cellular telephones continue to proliferate in places where land-based phone systems are rudimentary and unreliable or nonexistent. Air travel is used extensively throughout the world to establish direct and personal connections with faraway people and places. These and other developments in communication open many possibilities for real connections and real relationships within the global church family.

With these unprecedented possibilities of communication with virtually anyone anywhere, why do we not have more extensive, closer relationships among brother/sister churches in different parts of the world? The reasons are overlapping, but it can be helpful to separate them for the purpose of discussion. The most important of these obstacles to communication, relationships, and sharing gifts are the following:

- Economic differences
- Lack of administrative capacity
- Centralized decision making
- Lack of broad vision
- Fear of cultural, racial, theological, and other differences
- A view that some gifts are more valuable than others
- Greed

We will look briefly at each of these.

In many European and North American church structures which are otherwise well developed, little or no staffing is available for developing and maintaining relationships with other churches.

Economic Differences

The economic difference among people in different countries and different parts of the world is one of the most easily identifiable and most basic obstacles to healthy family relationships. Many member churches of our global church family simply do not have the financial resources necessary to establish basic communication with other churches: a land-based or cellular telephone, a computer, Internet access, or an electronic mail account. Other churches have the latest communications technology. These differences largely reflect the differences in relative material wealth among member churches.

Many statistics show that despite concerted national and international development efforts spanning three or four decades, and despite the promises of economic integration through globalization, the gap between the world's wealthy and the world's poor is increasing rather than decreasing. And long-term trends show that gulf continuing to widen. In 1820 this difference was 3-1; in 1950, 35-1; and in 1992, 72-1. As we know, a vast proportion of the world's wealth is controlled by a small number of individuals and corporations. In 1960 the richest 20% of the world's population had 30 times the income of the poorest 20%; in 1997 this had risen to 74 times. Several hundred of the world's wealthiest individuals own as much wealth as the world's 2.5 *billion* poorest people.

Such dramatic statistics often seem meaningless and unreal. These are global, secular statistics compiled by nameless people in obscure and distant offices. We can easily become immune to them and even deny that they have meaning for our global church family. There are no comprehensive statistics on economic wealth within our specific churches—for example, in the Dutch church, or the Colombian church—so we might argue that our church members are not typical, not as wealthy or not as poor as the national averages.

Of course this is a valid point. Each church has its own history and may come predominately from a wealthier or poorer section of the general population. But no one who has visited church offices in the Netherlands, the Congo, or Brazil, or worshiped in congregations in Canada, the Philippines, or Panama, or stayed in the homes of brothers and sisters in Kenya, Switzerland, or India can deny that there are indeed huge economic differences within the global family.

The headlines that often seem distant and unreal to us are in fact "family" headlines. Members of our family in Colombia are directly affected by war; members of our family in Zimbabwe are dying of AIDS; members in the U.S. have lost their employment; members in Indonesia are caught up in religious conflict.

We can find other ways to make some available statistics more real. Within our denominational family, we have roughly similar numbers of members in Zambia, Bolivia, and the Netherlands. Using national per capita Gross Domestic Product (GDP) statistics, we can say that the GDP of our Dutch church members collectively is about $280 million (U.S.). The equivalent figure for the Zambian church is about $4 million (U.S.) and for Bolivia $13 million (U.S.). The collective GDP of the Japanese churches with about 3,000 members is about five times as high as that of the 185,000 sisters and brothers in Congo. Using national averages, the 400,000 plus denominational sisters and brothers in all of Africa would have about the same number of computers as the 2,500 members of the Swiss church. We could go on. . . .

A final point to consider regarding economics is that a number of churches with long associations with mission agencies have been slow to develop and adapt the practice of self-support and stewardship. Outside subsidies in some cases led to an understanding that members did not need to support the church financially. As mission agencies moved on to other geographical areas, these churches had developed little means of financial support.

Lack of Administrative Capacity

When we think about our churches' administrative structures we have very different images, depending on where we are from. Within our family there are churches that have no administrative staff at all, while others have extensive offices and numerous administrators. Out of about 200 related church groups worldwide, 90 represent bodies of 500 members or less; 28 have over 10,000 members, and only eight have over 50,000. When we add to this mix the diverse socioeconomic climates in which these churches function, it becomes clear that there will be significant differences in churches' administrative capacities. Many of these churches are young, and any administrative capacity that is available is often heavily committed to internal issues and concerns.

Here again, general economic conditions play a significant role. We have visited church leaders for whom the logistics of general church oversight is a major preoccupation. Arranging transportation to visit outlying congregations can be a long and costly process. Even if there is a church vehicle, which is often not the case, it is not straightforward. Imagine general secretaries of national churches waiting in long lines for petrol or spending days tracking down spare parts or buying bus tickets. (This reality is a far cry from those church groups with permanent offices, in-house communication facilities, numerous staff, and funded administrative budgets.) In such conditions it is not surprising that the time available to work on sharing relationships with other churches is minimal. As long as these conditions prevail, it is hard to see how the isolation of smaller and economically challenged churches can be overcome.

The question of administrative capacity is not just an issue for younger churches. In many European and North American church structures which are otherwise well developed, little or no staffing is available for developing and maintaining relationships with other churches except within the mission agencies. This too is an impediment to the expansion of relationships and makes it difficult for congregations to find the support they need in order to develop sharing relationships with other churches.

Centralization of Decision Making

Sharing relationships between churches can and should be facilitated by the churches' decision-making structures, but those relationships must also be broadly owned by each church's grassroots. Gift sharing is first and foremost about recognizing and nurturing the gifts present as human resources within the church. These human resources are members of local congregations, and often it is the case that the greatest enthusiasm for direct sharing relationships is at the congregational level. This energy can easily be lost by an overly controlling church administration. The fine line between guidance and nurture on the one hand, and control and manipulation on the other, can be threatened by the desire of centralized church structures to maintain themselves. This is not only an issue for small churches where there is frequently one-person leadership—a president, a general secretary, a bishop. It is also a problem for large administrative structures which may see congregational activism as a threat for a variety of reasons. At the same time, congregations may find such structures distant and inaccessible.

We have encountered a number of examples of gifts that are obstructed in this way. Once a congregation approached us with their plans to create a partnership with a congregation in another country. They had a lot of enthusiasm and the congregation was excited about the possibilities. We offered some suggestions and gave some counsel and encouraged them to be in touch with their conference offices. When the conference offices heard of the ideas, they told the congregation that their plans needed to be processed "internally." We have since learned that nothing further has happened with this congregational initiative.

In another setting, a young woman pastor agreed to take responsibility for planning and organizing a gathering of women pastors and theologians from several conferences in the region. Together with other women from her church she developed an exciting program for the proposed meeting. But the male leadership of her conference ultimately decided that the women of the conference could not participate in the program, and the gathering had to be moved at the last minute to a neighboring country.

We should be clear: a real commitment to the nurture of gifts within the church and to sharing those gifts with others calls for strong organization and leadership by church officials. But sharing relationships cannot happen when church structures are concerned about control. The enthusiasm that exists for sharing gifts must be given encouragement and space to develop, explore, and evolve.

Lack of Broad Vision

Earlier in this book we have written of God's vision of abundant life for all which can only be made possible through open sharing. This same vision must be the clear and present priority of every church. When it is lost or moved from the forefront of the churches' purpose, the enthusiasm, and indeed the possibility, for sharing gifts will be lost with it.

Of course it is important for every church to be internally strong. It is important that each member experience acceptance and comfort in a local congregation. For this to happen, leaders, pastors, and members need to give constant attention to the internal health of the whole congregation. But to what end? Certainly not so that a congregation or a church can be strong enough to go it alone, not so that the church or congregation can function in isolation, making sure that its members are wrapped comfortably in a cocoon. The ultimate vision for

The fear of difference stands in the way of sharing gifts.

the church at any level, the local congregation as well as the national conference, is always global in its view. The promise of abundant life is for all, for the whole world. And this can only be accomplished when all members of the church are actively equipped to go out and share the gifts they have been given.

Most of us are familiar with churches that have a strong internal focus, that consume much of their energy putting their house in order, taking care of the needs of members, and making sure that church is "a good experience" for those who attend on Sunday morning. One is reminded of the passage in Matthew and Luke where, in response to Jesus's invitation, "Follow me!" a man says, "Lord, first let me go and bury my father." Jesus's reply seems harsh ("Let the dead bury their own dead"), but his point is clear. There will always be good reasons to put off the work that is to be done, the life we are called to lead. Minding our own affairs does not prepare us for sharing our gifts with others, for following Jesus to the abundant life.

Fear of Cultural, Racial, Theological, and Other Differences

Elsewhere in this book we have suggested that God's creation functions through the intricate interaction and interrelationships of differences. The Apostle Paul's well-known metaphor of the body, in the I Corinthians passage to which we have already made reference, illustrates the complex dialogue in each of our lives between sameness and difference, between one and many. The writer seems to be making two contradictory points: "though we are many, yet we are one."

Perhaps it is true for all people, even for all of life, that the way we live with this tension, this dialectic, is one of our most basic and formative themes. We could say, both metaphorically and actually, that it has to do with the dual desires to leave home and to return home; to go away and to come back. Walter Burkert in his book *Creation of the Sacred* refers to this phenomenon as the "quest" theme and shows how the basic pattern of going out and coming back is universal to folk tales and mythology in unrelated human social settings all over the world. To different degrees and in different ways we all experience the longing for likeness, for the familiar, for the comfort of the known, just as we are drawn by the challenge, the excitement of what is foreign, strange, unknown, and different.

God's vision of abundant living, like Jesus' invitation to "Follow me," is not a call to abandon home, the comfort of the known. Rather it is an invitation to share what is "home" to us with others and also to share with others what is "home" to them. As a result, our "home" expands and changes and becomes a place of comfort and support for others as well.

In this section we suggest that the fear of difference stands in the way of sharing gifts. The reasons for these fears—of someone of a different nationality, different beliefs, a different race, a different culture, a different class—are many and varied. What is important to understand, as we have maintained throughout this book, is that differences are gifts to us from God. In welcoming them and sharing in them we make it possible for our own gifts to flourish. In fearing and isolating ourselves from them, we impede God's vision for abundant life.

A View that Some Gifts Are More Valuable Than Others

In Luke 22:24 we read:

> A dispute also arose among them as to which one of them was to be regarded as the greatest. But he said to them, "The kings of the Gentiles lord it over them; and those in authority over them are called benefactors. But not so with you; rather the greatest among you must become like the youngest, and the leader like one who serves. For who is greater, the one who is at the table or the one who serves? Is it not the one at the table? But I am among you as one who serves.

Here Jesus recognizes that there is a social and political hierarchy in the world, but that there is not to be one among his followers: "*But not so with you . . .*" It is hard to imagine how Jesus could say this more clearly. His consistent response to questions about who is best or highest is to "become like children," or to be "servant of all." Likewise, Paul's writing on gifts in both I Corinthians and Romans seems specifically to address a discussion within the church about which gifts are higher or more important than others:

> . . . I say to everyone among you not to think of yourself more highly than you ought to think, but to think with sober judgment, each according to the measure of faith that God has assigned. For as in one body we have many members, and not all the members have the same function, so we, who are many, are one body in Christ, and individually we are members one of another (Romans 12:3-5).

In spite of these clear words against the lifting up of one gift above others, in many churches certain gifts are recognized and honored while others are ignored. This has resulted in many people thinking that they have no gifts that are of value to the church and thus nothing to share with others. This, too, is an obstacle to God's sharing purpose.

Greed

Greed is defined as "an all-consuming acquisitiveness." In Colossians Paul calls it idolatry, because the overpowering wish to possess something elevates the thing desired to the place of God. Greed is the rejection of sharing, and, as one writer says, it "destroys the 'communitarian' purpose of the universe."

No one that we know of has seriously argued the case for greed. However, many people do expend much energy accumulating wealth or power over others. II Corinthians 8 and 9 treat the questions of wealth and sharing quite directly. Note some of the interesting aspects of Paul's case to the Corinthians for generosity and sharing:

- Paul cites the example of the Macedonian churches, whose "extreme poverty" overflowed in a "wealth of generosity" (8:2).
- Sharing is a "privilege" (8:4).
- Jesus's example ("though he was rich, yet for your sakes he became poor") is cited as a "generous act," the opposite of greed (8:9).
- Abundance and need are linked together. This makes it clear that wealth is meant to be shared. Paul makes the case for a "fair balance" among everyone (8:14).
- The same point is made again, even more clearly, when Paul says that "God is able to provide you with every blessing in abundance, so that by always having enough of everything, you may share abundantly in every good work" (9:8).

The imbalance in the distribution of material wealth in the world has already been noted above. We need to ask ourselves what it means that this imbalance is mirrored within the church.

We raise this question with some reluctance, because our emphasis on sharing gifts in the global church must not be reduced to a euphemism for calling upon those with material gifts to share with those with material needs. Indeed, our central claim from the beginning has been that we have *all* been given gifts, that we *all* need each others' gifts, and that God intends that *all* of us share our gifts.

Nevertheless, we think there are four primary reasons why the imbalance of material wealth must be specifically addressed in any discussion of sharing gifts. First, the accumulation of wealth and material things has long been recognized as a particular temptation or problem for human beings. It was singled out for repeated critique by the Old Testament prophets and by Jesus.

Second, as we have noted, the world seems clearly to be moving further away from, rather than towards, the "fair balance" to which Paul refers.

Third, while material gifts should not have a privileged position, most of us at some time or another have material needs that stand in the way of developing gifts we have, material and otherwise, that we would like to share. We recall an example of this point from our workshop with a South African church. There, one of the youngest participants in all the workshops we held, a 14- year-old boy, had been chosen to attend because he was recognized in the church as having a special artistic gift. The church made use of his gifts by asking him to create banners and drawings whenever these were needed by the church. His dream was to continue his education and eventually attend art school. Unfortunately, he was from a poor, single-parent family and had already been forced to drop out of secondary school for lack of money for school fees.

Fourth, and perhaps most importantly, people with material wealth are also part of the global family. Their participation in the family is important, and they, too, have needs which the family should meet. Material wealth can insulate us from each other. It can prevent us from forming the kinds of relationships with each other on which the health of both individual members and the body, the family, depends.

During a training session for workshop facilitators in Latin America, a number of the women facilitators voiced their concerns about how they would be received in churches where women traditionally have few leadership roles. After visiting several churches in Mexico, one facilitator wrote:

> "Do you remember the fears that we expressed in relation to leadership of women? Well, in the two places I had marvelous experiences. In Chihuahua I preached two times

in the morning and in the afternoon on Sunday, in two different churches. Quite something, isn't it? In Sinaloa, at the end of the workshop an elderly sister asked that they pray for me, and she told the men, leaders, and pastors to lay their hands on me. One of them gave a prayer as if he knew my life; the prayer was exact. For me it was a recognition of my ministry and a blessing, a gift that they and the Lord gave me that was marvelous."

The churches we visited in Angola have throughout nearly their entire existence operated in a context of war. As a result, one would not automatically think of Angola as a place where many gifts could be found for sharing. But we observed there churches that took very seriously their responsibilities within their communities, particularly in the area of education. Dynamic primary and secondary schools, as well as health training schools, are part of the church's involvements. It was also in Angola that one church leader suggested that the desperate social needs of Angolans themselves could be understood as potential gifts. He suggested that one thing they could share with churches in other places is the opportunity to partner with the Angolan church in responding to the needs of former child soldiers in Angola.

This brings us back to where we started this chapter. The obstacles to gift sharing are many and formidable. But when we recognize the need for each member of the family and nurture our natural enthusiasm for relationships with others who are different, the difficulties can be borne and the obstacles surmounted.

6.
A Gift Sharing Church

If you remove the yoke from among you,
the pointing of the finger, the speaking of evil,
if you offer your food to the hungry
and satisfy the needs of the afflicted,
then your light shall rise in the darkness
and your gloom be like the noonday.
The Lord will guide you continually,
and satisfy your needs in parched places,
and make your bones strong;
and you shall be like a watered garden, like a spring of water,
whose waters never fail.

(Isaiah 58:9-11)

To this point we have discussed gifts themselves and how they are related to needs, what sharing is, the biblical understanding of gifts, where they come from, and their purpose in the world. We have discussed the global church family and God's intention of abundant life for all.

Finally, we have also considered some of the obstacles which often stand in the way of sharing of gifts. We note that while these barriers are substantial and formidable, they are not the last word. Churches everywhere are energized by the idea that they have gifts that can be shared with others who are in different circumstances, just as they are eager to receive the gifts of sisters and brothers elsewhere, and to build closer relationships with them through sharing. In this chapter we want to look concretely at how gift sharing relationships can be developed between congregations and between churches.

Discovering Our Gifts

Perhaps the first step in becoming a church which shares its gifts is for the church to become fully aware of itself as a body to which God has entrusted certain gifts, which are in turn meant to be shared. A church which doesn't believe it is gifted will have little to share with others, just as a church which sees gifts as private matters for individual use will not be able to join in God's vision of abundant living. It is the responsibility of church leadership to establish a climate which gives priority to identifying and nurturing gifts. We can think of no better guide in this than Paul's message in I Corinthians 12:23-25:

> . . . those members of the body that we think less honorable we clothe with greater honor, and our less respectable members are treated with greater respect; whereas our more respectable members do not need this. But God has so arranged the body, giving the greater honor to the inferior member, that there may be no dissension within the body, but the members may have the same care for one another.

Who are the people in your church whose gifts are unacknowledged? Youth? Elderly? Women? People of a particular region or ethnicity? Those with less formal education? These

A church which doesn't believe it is gifted will have little to share with others, just as a church which sees gifts as private matters for individual use will not be able to join in God's vision of abundant living.

are the persons we are called to "clothe with greater honor." And that can be done authentically only by believing that they, too, are gifted and by identifying and nurturing their gifts.

Because churches are living beings which change as their members themselves grow and change, and as they gain and lose members, discerning gifts needs to be an ongoing process. Gift discernment can and should happen in many different ways and at different levels. Let us note some of these:

1. The leaders of our churches—officials, pastors, deacons— need to see each member as a sacred trust to the church through whom God is sharing particular gifts. As persons with authority and power, they should be attentive to all occasions in which that authority can be used to lift up others. This means inviting others to share responsibilities and leadership.

2. The educational institutions of our churches should be teaching those who are being trained for pastoral, evangel-

istic, and other leadership roles about how to elicit and nurture the gifts of others. Our Bible schools and seminaries teach preaching, worship leading, and evangelism strategies. Discerning and nurturing gifts are equally important skills for future leaders.

3. National conferences should consider ways of maintaining deliberate and regular discovery of the gifts of their members. This might be done by establishing gift discernment as a formal part of the conference's structure, by holding regular gift sharing workshops, or by creating and maintaining a conference register of special gifts.

4. A similar focus on gifts should be initiated at the congregational level. Congregations might encourage the giving of a diversity of gifts, rather than only material gifts, in their regular Sunday offerings.

5. We should look for ways to formalize the understanding that to be a part of the church family is to share gifts. A declaration of the gifts we are committed to sharing might be made a part of the service of baptism for new members, or of Holy Communion for continuing members. Likewise, conferences that apply for membership to worldwide denominational bodies might be asked to declare the gifts that they bring to the broader church.

6. In some situations the best way to become more aware of the gifts we have to offer is to examine our needs. Our genuine needs are always signs of gifts which want to be expressed and released. If we feel that we have no needs we will find it difficult to enter into sharing relationships with others.

Through such measures we can begin to imagine what it means to be part of a global church family who takes seriously the gifts God has shared with us and who is prepared to share these gifts with other members of the family. Through all of this we should keep in mind that the purpose of this sharing is the building of our interrelatedness and the abundant life which Jesus offers us.

Becoming Part of the Family

Earlier we have written about some of the differences which keep us from functioning as a global church family. What are the practical ways in which these differences can be overcome? We want to look in particular at how churches which are preoccupied with fundamental survival needs, whose gifts are obstructed by chronic economic crises, enter into genuine sharing relationships with materially wealthy churches, and vice versa.

When we began our work with Global Gift Sharing, we were told that the program would involve human resources and that money, cash, would be excluded. One of the first changes which we brought to the original proposal was to reverse this exclusion and to insist that no gift—including money—should be automatically excluded. To include money as a gift that can be shared does make things more difficult, because, as we have mentioned earlier, money resists attachment and is, of all potential gifts, the least relational. Yet it cannot be denied that financial resources are an important gift which some members of the family have, and that money can clearly be used to enable and release other gifts. We believe that it is an appropriate challenge for the global church family to try to discover how this gift, too, can be shared in ways which build stronger relationships between different parts of the body.

As a point of departure, we believe it is important that there be an acknowledgment by all parts of the church family that this is an issue which we need to discuss openly together. We feel free to discuss other gifts and needs in the global church-for example, how the gifts of women can be better used in the churches, or how a conference with a particular vision and particular gifts for cross-cultural mission might be most useful to the broader church, or how we ought to respond to a famine, war, or earthquake that affects part of the body. In the same way, the question of how a church with significant financial resources can relate to other parts of the family should be a general concern that can be discussed.

At the same time, we should recognize that every church has some degree of financial means, and in every social context there are some individuals who have more money than others. It is important that no part of the church be stereotyped as "wealthy" or "poor," just as none should be seen to have a corner on hospitality, spirituality, or musical ability. Thus, the discussion about wealth in the church should be a global discussion with specific relevance in each conference, even each congregation, rather than a conversation that focuses only on one part of the worldwide church.

It would be a significant step forward if the church could clearly recognize the "gift status" of money. Sometimes those who are materially wealthy are made to feel apologetic for that fact, or to feel that their gift is somehow less "spiritual" than others. In fact, there are a variety of distinct gifts related to money that ought to be recognized, such as the gift of creating employment opportunities, of small business skills, of the management of finances, investment, and giving, and so on. Giving "gift status" to money might open up new space to consider how it can be shared more fully and more appropriately in the global family.

"The Lord will guide you continually, and satisfy your needs in parched places, and make your bones strong."

We emphasize that we are concerned about *sharing* rather than simply *giving*. What does it mean to share a gift of money? In short, money, like other gifts, should be used to build relationships, which in turn free and nurture other gifts. Sharing money means that both parties are involved and have a vested interest in the activity. Those with whom money is shared need to use it in ways which respect the relationship, which recognize that the spirit of the person or persons sharing is a part of the gift, and which support the understanding that money is a "spiritual gift" in the sense that it ultimately comes from God, just like all other gifts.

When money is understood by all of us as a special gift of God, like many other gifts, it then becomes possible to understand the Apostle Paul's words in II Corinthians 8 and 9, where he says that sharing wealth is a "privilege" (8:4), not something that is done "reluctantly or under compulsion" (9:7). Sharing wealth is a way of helping others to have the privilege of sharing gifts by contributing to the nurture of their gifts.

Again, sharing within the family is not about making everyone equal. It is about freeing and nurturing the gifts of the other through relationship. This is true whether the gift being shared is preaching or teaching or singing or food or money or computer skills.

Our membership in the family can happen by birth (blood) or through adoption. But we truly become a part through sharing our gifts. There is no other way.

Local and Global

Our subject in this book is the sharing of gifts in the worldwide church. We have noted that many people, congregations, and churches are particularly energized by the prospect of sharing with people and groups who are very different and, in a sense, exotic. In many ways this is a good thing. Because distance tends to isolate us from each other, it is particularly important that we work hard to develop and maintain relationships with people and churches far away from us. Distance is also often a cause of marginalization, and our faith asks us to carry a special concern for those who are marginalized and seen as less important. Global relationships can enlarge our understanding and enrich our lives.

At the same time, the foundation for sharing in the global church is sharing locally. In a family, home is the place where values like sharing are modeled, taught, and learned. An awareness of gifts, and sharing of them, should be an integral part of the internal life of every congregation. We will share most naturally and regularly with the brothers and sisters who are physically closest to us.

We have often seen that sharing gifts works well between churches in the same region. Two years ago we held a Gift Sharing workshop for the countries of Ghana and Burkina Faso. Although they are neighbors, representatives from these churches had never come together before. There was no common language for the two groups, so we conducted the workshop with translation throughout. After the meeting a group of Ghanaian women came to us saying that they wanted to send a delegation to the women of Burkina Faso to teach them how to make gari. The process involves a method of preserving cassava which is widely used in Ghana but not well known in Burkina. Because it involved neighboring churches, this shared activity was feasible.

A similar gift sharing activity took place between churches in Costa Rica and Panama, described here by Sandra Campos, a Gift Sharing facilitator in Costa Rica:

> This past January I received an invitation to participate in a training workshop with a group of brothers and sisters from different countries in Latin America and to be a facilitator for the Global Gift Sharing program. My task was to lead workshops in Panama and Costa Rica.
>
> In the month of March I made a preliminary visit to Panama in order to become more familiar with the context of the church. During this visit I was impressed by the skillful handicraft work of the Panamanian brothers and sisters and by the fact that their main source of income is generated from this activity. As a result, when I returned to Costa Rica I proposed to my church that they support the expenses of one of our members, Sister Elena Carvajal, to accompany me in April on my second visit to Panama to hold the Gift Sharing workshop, so that she could teach the Panamanian brothers and sisters "Dry Art," which is the

making of greeting cards and bookmarks using dried flowers and leaves.

The proposal was well received by the Costa Rican church, and so this past April we went together to Panama City. Sister Elena held a workshop in which 12 women and one man participated with great enthusiasm. At the conclusion of the workshop we shared an outdoor supper together. To celebrate this sharing of gifts between Costa Rica and Panama we sang a hymn in which the final verse says:

New people, loving without borders,
beyond race and place,
New people, on the side of the poor,
Sharing with them shelter and food.

This experience is only the beginning of gift sharing, as the people of the Panama church hope that Elena will return. They have also expressed interest in having Costa Rica assist them with initiating a youth ministry. The Panamanian and Costa Rican brothers and sisters thank God for this experience.

Regional sharing experiences such as these are often more practical and less costly than those done over greater distances. As a result, it is easier to maintain connections and continue a relationship over an extended period of time.

The Sharing Church

A sharing church, a global church family. What does it look like? What kind of vision guides it? We imagine geographically dispersed communities, speaking different languages, worshiping with different styles, living in diverse socio-economic conditions, but sharing a common understanding of God's incarnational purpose of abundant life for all people, for the entire world. We see a church in the Philippines which, as it works toward this purpose in its local setting, calls on gifts of all kinds from sisters and brothers in Panama and in Italy. We see a Bible school in Zambia that welcomes students, teachers, and books from churches in Namibia and India and Canada. We see a consultant from Congo advising a congregation's building committee in the U.S. We see a youth program in Mexico with volunteers from Angola and Indonesia. We see a church with many gifts, many relationships, and with one spirit, one purpose.

But let us consider the question in more detail, in more specific terms. Sharing gifts with each other or among churches— these are creative acts, creative engagements, and we do not want to outline models that must be followed, or policies and procedures, or do's and don't's. At the same time, our creativity can often be stimulated and encouraged by a broader awareness of what others have done.

Church sharing relationships can take place at different levels. One is between national churches or conferences. Another is between district or regional structures of different national conferences. A third is among two or more congregations. Yet another is between church institutions—Bible schools, hospitals, secondary schools, social programs, publishing houses, and so on. Each of these has its unique value and purpose. What is of ultimate importance is that in every case the focus should be on creating opportunities for personal connections and relationships between people— whether they are church leaders, pastors, institutional leaders, or people in the pews. Let us look at each of these levels briefly and try to imagine some of the sharing relationships that might take place.

National Conferences. Historically the formal relationships among national conferences within denominations have been of a limited and prescribed type. Many churches have strong historic connections to the churches that were instrumental in initiating and/or nurturing them. But these relationships have almost always been between a church and an agency rather than between the two churches directly. As a result, initiating churches often find themselves with no direct relationship to churches they have supported for many years, and younger churches find themselves linked not to a church but to a specialized agency, which historically mediates relationships with other parts of the denominational family.

Both churches and mission/service agencies want to move beyond these patterns and find new agency definitions and

A declaration of the gifts we are committed to sharing might be made a part of the service of baptism for new members, or of Holy Communion for continuing members.

new models for church to church relationship. It is thus an opportune time for churches at the conference or national level to explore ways to make external or inter-church relations a significant, integral part of what the church is and does. We believe it is appropriate for conferences in all parts of the worldwide church to establish specific goals for developing relationships with other conferences.

How should this happen? First, churches need to think about why relationships with other churches are important and necessary. Like all other objectives of a church, the goal of relationships with other churches should be based in a clearly articulated, theologically based vision. Second, it is important for a church to make sure that adequate administrative resources are available to undertake new relationships. This is not necessarily a call for new departments and staffing, but relationships are a lot of work. One should not expect that new partnerships can be formed with other churches without anyone taking specific responsibility, and without administrative time and energy being made available for this purpose.

Third, it is important for a church to think through in a general way what its gifts are and what its strengths are; in short, what it might bring to a partnership with another conference. Equally important, the church should identify areas in which it is looking for help from others. Recently we visited with churches in the Netherlands. Major concerns of the church there are low church attendance, the lack of liveliness in worship styles, and, in general, the effect of secularization on the church. As a result the conference has set out deliberately to develop relationships with several African churches. One part of this initiative was a visit by a group of African women to the Netherlands. The mission department of the church also sent a musician to Zambia to collect hymns used by the churches in Africa. "We felt it would be a good way to introduce more liveliness and diversity into our worship," a Dutch pastor explained.

Fourth, a church conference should then consider which other church or churches should be approached for partnership. There are many different factors that can enter into such a decision. Among these are:

- how difficult will it be to sustain a relationship over time (issues of language, distance, common interests, complementary gifts, etc.)
- is there a common history, and is this seen as a positive or a negative factor
- are there natural connections between the two churches—such as significant numbers of people from one of the churches who have spent time with the other church
- is it possible to envision potential matches between gifts, needs, and opportunities in the respective churches

There is a certain awkwardness about one church "choosing" another church for a relationship; ideally such relationships would grow naturally from contact among churches. However, in many cases there are few occasions for such natural connections. The process could be made more authentic by involving an international denominational or ecumenical body which has connections to churches in different parts of the world.

What could be the substance of a relationship between two national conferences? There are numerous possibilities:

- exchange visits of leaders and others
- representation at the annual assemblies of the partner churches
- "shadowing" by people in equivalent positions—for example the youth director of one conference could

spend a week following in the steps of the youth director
of the partner conference
- collaboration on joint projects such as curriculum development, historical writing, social programs
- sending/receiving students to/from partner educational
institutions
- the establishment of a general understanding to encourage congregational level relationships and connections

A group of Honduran church leaders was invited to visit the
Dutch churches as a step toward a partner relationship between
the two conferences. Toward the end of the visit, we asked the
Hondurans what they found interesting or different about the
churches in the Netherlands. "We found that the Dutch have a
deeply rooted historical understanding of the church, and one
aspect of this is a strong congregational autonomy. In Honduras
the missionaries brought a much more centralized structure."
Another aspect which impressed the visitors was the attitude of
respect for different approaches and beliefs. The Hondurans
were surprised by the way baptism was done in the Dutch
churches. "Here you are baptized when you create your own
personal confession of faith—sometimes it is not even written in
words, but acted out or presented graphically. In Honduras we
all use the same confession of faith for baptism." The
Hondurans would like to see some "twinning" relationships
established between Honduran and Dutch congregations. "We
believe that there could be a lot of sharing on how to do pastoral care and different styles of worship."

Ultimately a relationship between national conferences can
rarely be sustained at that level alone. It is usually necessary
for congregations to become involved by making their own
connections and relationships with congregations in the partner conference. This adds another important question to the

Sharing within the family is not about making everyone equal. It is about freeing and nurturing the gifts of the other through relationship.

process of selecting partners for relationships—will congregations be ready to become involved?

District/Regional Structures. In many denominational groups there is no standardized regional structure from one national conference to the next. In addition, there is often great variation in terms of the overall size of national conferences. In such a reality, it is easy for smaller churches to be excluded from relationships. One way to address this problem would be for district or regional structures of a large conference to have relationships with smaller national conferences. In a similar way, national conferences of comparable size could match districts or regions of each church for more grassroots relational activity.

Congregational Relationships. Most of the relationships that exist across national conference lines are congregationally based. However, apart from formal "sister church" programs, many of the current congregational relationships represent initiatives taken by one congregation without any specific congregational focus in a partner national conference. Many focus on a specific task—building a church or a school, refurbishing a building, or being involved in an evangelistic campaign. Once completed, there is little to sustain the relationship.

We believe that it would be a healthy thing for many congregational initiatives to be based on congregation to congregation relationships. This would encourage more sustained connections, and also make it possible to avoid the one-way sharing that can easily result from a task-oriented relationship.

There are a number of different programs which have the primary objective of church to church relationships. As a result, quite a bit of work has been done to analyze what kinds of activities are most effective in fostering strong relationships. One sister church program initiated by the Mennonite churches in Colombia lists the following primary purposes and activities:

1. Mutual understanding and relationship: each church is asked to provide a short history and profile of their congregation and its local context which may include photos, letters, creative works, contributions from both the adult and children's Sunday school classes, etc.

2. Prayer: use email and other mediums of communication to share thanksgivings, petitions, and, hopefully, responses to prayer. "For no one can lay any foundation other than the one that has been laid; that foundation is Jesus Christ" (I Corinthians 3 :11).

3. Exchanges/visits: facilitate the possibility of receiving visits from church members and pastors in both directions in

order to exchange pulpits and know one another personally.

4. Sharing gifts: some examples might include sending creative works, sharing teachers, volunteer workers, or educational resources.

5. Sharing resources: This relationship should not be looked at from the perspective of economic interests. As with a familial relationship between sisters it should not depend on or revolve around an economic relationship. Nevertheless, possibilities of economic support of a sister church for a local church project may emerge. These projects will have to be created in partnership with the local Colombian church and meet their approval, as well as that of the regional and national committees that oversee them. If the project is approved, the investment of funds will be done under the supervision of the regional committee.

6. Lobbying-defense of human rights: intervene before the government, both Colombian and foreign, in defense of people, churches, and policies. Oppose damaging and harmful policies. Grow together in an awareness of global justice.

It is important to keep in mind that a congregation to congregation relationship has the potential to empower both congregations to better carry out ministry in the world. This is the ultimate purpose of relationship. It should not be expected that a sister-church relationship itself should consume the gifts and resources of the congregations involved. On the contrary, the relationship is the vehicle by which gifts should be empowered and released to other situations and other contexts. If a congregation feels that it cannot become involved in a particular response because all of its resources are being used in a sister-church relationship, probably that relationship should be carefully reviewed.

Institutional Relationships. Connections between parallel institutions of different conferences are sometimes among the easiest relationships to develop. Unlike congregations, institutions such as Bible schools, universities, healthcare facilities, and service programs have relatively sophisticated administrative structures which can accommodate incoming or outgoing human and other resources, and which can maintain a relationship over a period of time. In addition, because such institutions have relatively specific goals, it is easy to define the terms of the relationship with some clarity. Once again we feel that institutional relationships can be most fruitful in the context of a broader conference partnership.

Among the kinds of activities that can be envisioned in relationships between institutions are the sharing of special curricula that may have been developed in specialized areas, the sharing of teachers or professors, sending and receiving Bible school or university students from other churches, translating and publishing materials that have been written in a different church context, issuing joint degrees, placing medical interns and other health personnel in training or teaching capacities, etc.

An anthropologist quoted a southern African Bushman who explained his community's attitude toward sharing by saying, "If people do not like each other but one gives a gift and the other must accept, this brings a peace between them. We give what we have. That is the way we live together." That simple, clear statement is what God intends for all of us. By sharing what we have, what God has shared with us, it is possible for us to live together—as a global family.

7.

Being Rich Toward God

Who then will offer willingly,
consecrating themselves today to the Lord?

(I Chronicles 29:5)

As we have visited churches around the world we have seen
everywhere the great wealth of the church. There are churches
with much or with little material wealth, but all churches have
many human resources, people with God-given gifts. Our task
has been to discover together ways that these gifts can be
released.

In Luke 12 there is an interesting parable about using wealth
or gifts. We are told that a man in the crowd wanted Jesus to
make his brother share the family inheritance with him. After a
warning about greed, Jesus told this story:

> The land of a rich man produced abundantly. And he
> thought to himself, "What should I do, for I have no place to
> store my crops?" Then he said, "I will do this: I will pull down
> my barns and build larger ones, and there I will store all my
> grain and my goods. And I will say to my soul, 'Soul, you have
> ample goods laid up for many years; relax, eat, drink, be
> merry.'" But God said to him, "You fool! This very night your
> life is being demanded of you. And the things you have pre-

pared, whose will they be?" So it is with those who store up treasures for themselves but are not rich toward God.

Sometimes it may seem that our churches, in both a real and a figurative sense, are storehouses of wealth—places where human resources are collected and stored, sometimes in ever larger "barns." Jesus contrasts keeping our gifts to ourselves with being "rich toward God." For a church to be rich toward God, the gifts under the stewardship of the church must be released.

There are many different ways this can happen. But the initial step must always be an acknowledgment and awareness of the gifts we have and an understanding that they have been given to us by God to be shared.

Gift discernment is nothing new. There are many congregations that are already sensitized to the importance of this activity for the church, and that have developed ways to identify and nurture gifts among their members. The gift sharing program that has inspired this writing has functioned through one- or two-day workshops at the level of national church conferences. Usually the workshops were made up of a group of 20-30 people chosen by church leadership to represent the church as a whole. But as the following account suggests, this is not always the best approach:

"I don't mean to be difficult, but could you tell us in simple language—in one sentence—what this program is trying to do?" The two of us were in Strasbourg, France, meeting with a group of people who had been sent by the European churches to be trained as Global Gift Sharing facilitators. It was the first time we had attempted to do the training program in the "global North." We had assumed some of the issues and questions would be different, but we hadn't known in what ways that would be so.

So this question from one of the participants caught us off guard, partly because it came near the end of the day after we had spent several hours in lively discussion about the theoretical aspects of gifts, sharing, and biblical foundations. We had just come to the part where we asked people to divide up in groups and make a plan for how they would do Gift Sharing workshops in each national church.

I don't recall how we answered the question—something about building relationships between churches—but it wasn't clear enough, wasn't tangible enough or specific enough, and the workshop fizzled to a close shortly after.

This question, too, was a gift. It served to remind us of the very different cultures of churches around the world. It reminded us that we need to look constantly for ways to make the nurturing, facilitative model more concrete and easily understood.

In some situations the identification of gifts can best be done at a conference or a district level. In a conference with many congregations (and anywhere from several hundred to a hundred thousand members), it would be difficult for one small group to identify the gifts of the whole church. In this book we have emphasized that every person has valuable gifts, and no one's gifts should be ignored or taken lightly. It is therefore understandable that in almost every workshop we have done, participants have said that similar workshops should take place at the congregational level. In some churches it may be practical to use small group or Sunday school class structures to focus on gifts.

At the conclusion of a workshop in the Philippines, a leader suggested that "there should be a team of teachers who will go to all the churches to teach about gifts. This would be more effective than simply having resident pastors preach on the subject."

Suggestions for Congregations

Following are some suggestions that might be useful for congregations that want to initiate a gift sharing and discernment process. These should be adapted to fit the congregation or group concerned. It is good to experiment with approaches that reflect the creativity of the congregation.

Regardless of the approach used, there should be a clear focus on the key premises of the biblical understanding of gifts which have been highlighted throughout this book. We can summarize these as follows:

- All gifts come from God and have their origin in God's creative work.
- God intends abundant life for all through the interrelationship of all life. Gifts are shared to fulfill this purpose.
- Every person has gifts that are useful and necessary for God's plan or purpose.
- God *shares* gifts with us rather than simply gives gifts to us; in this way God's desire to be in ongoing relationship with creation is demonstrated.
- When we share our gifts with sisters and brothers we build relationships with them and make it possible for them to share their gifts with others.

The goal of focusing on gift sharing is to make congregations and individual members more aware of their gifts and to make them more eager and willing to share them with others. How can this best be achieved? Here are several steps:

Choosing a structure. As noted above, a variety of ways can encourage greater awareness of gifts at the level of the congregation. Whether through a congregational workshop, Sunday school class, small group, congregational retreat, or written surveys, the approach chosen should be adapted to the congregation and allow the greatest possible participation.

Participation. It would be ideal for everyone in the congregation—young and old—to be involved in gift discernment. If this is not practical, then it is important to have as representative a group as possible focusing on the gifts within the congregation. Earlier in this book we stressed the importance of diversity. The more representative the group is of the variety within the congregation, the better the possibility that many different gifts can be identified and expressed.

Content. We have included some aids for gift discernment as appendices to this book. Many other writings on gift discernment are also available.

Results of discernment process. The most important result of a gift discernment process is a greater awareness of the gifts of each member of the congregation. This might be something that could be formalized in an actual "inventory" of gifts. In addition, the process should result in an understanding that nurturing the gifts of members is one of the most important functions of the congregation. Identifying gifts is not a one-time process but an ongoing commitment, involving careful attention to changing gifts and needs.

Once a congregation is better in touch with its gifts and the gifts of its members, it is then important to find ways that these gifts can be shared. To identify gifts without using (sharing) them is an empty, lifeless process. Many people find their own ways of sharing gifts, but others need the help and counsel of sisters and brothers. In addition, there are some sharing activities that should be done by the congregation as a whole. The sharing of gifts both individually and as a group should be an ongoing preoccupation of every congregation.

"How can churches in one place get in touch with churches in other places?" This practical question came up many times during our visits. A church in Kenya said they would like to see a directory of women/youth leaders and programs in the different churches in Africa. In Latin America people spoke of the need for a central data base of gifts.

There is no fixed recipe for the faithful sharing of the gifts which God has entrusted to us. But at the same time, the church should not assume that gift sharing will just happen on its own without any encouragement, facilitation, and ongoing teaching. There should be structures both at the congregational and the conference level to encourage and facilitate these sharing initiatives and relationships. The church needs to play an active role in supporting and building relationships of sharing within the worldwide family. This is the way that we can enrich each other with the awareness of and participation in God's purpose of interrelatedness for all of life. It is the way that our many gifts find the same spirit. It is the way all of God's children can live together.

Appendices

The following pieces may help stimulate discussion about gifts and sharing at the congregational level. They emphasize ideas and issues that have been discussed in this book and that we have used in many different parts of the worldwide church. They may be freely copied for use in congregational settings.

What Do We Mean by "Gift?"

There are many different definitions of "gift," and it would be difficult to establish any fixed understanding about what is and what is not a gift. Our hope is that we can learn together of the wide diversity of gifts that God has bestowed upon us as individuals, as the church, and the world as a whole. Participants are encouraged to think expansively of different kinds and categories of gifts.

Within the church we often think only of "spiritual gifts" which Paul refers to in I Corinthians: wisdom, knowledge, faith, healing, miracles, prophecy, discernment, speaking in and interpreting tongues. However, this list is neither comprehensive nor hierarchical. The Bible affirms time and again that God is the source of all gifts, and Paul himself in I Corinthians 12 speaks strongly against a hierarchy of gifts. It is important for the church to identify and give honour to the diversity of gifts of each person. As Paul states in I Corinthians 7:7, ". . . each has a particular gift from God, one having one kind and another a different kind." Given that all gifts come from God, all gifts are spiritual.

As a guide for thinking about different gifts, the following list of general kinds of gifts may be a useful starting point:

1. *Gifts of creation* including all of the elements and creatures of the natural world.
2. *Gifts of special skills and aptitudes*—capacities and talents which different individuals possess.
3. *Gifts of insight and inspiration*—unique abilities to express and clarify what others cannot easily see or understand.
4. *Material Gifts*—money, goods of all kinds.
5. *Relational Gifts*—abilities to respond to and nurture people's relational needs.

Gifts are things (words, thoughts, objects, services) that are given and/or received. There is almost no limit to what may be considered a gift—an aptitude, talent, skill, material object, thought, task, time, prayer, or song. All these can be gifts when they are given in love and concern for the other.

What Is the Relationship Between Gifts and Needs?

The relationship between gifts and needs is one of the most difficult, as well as one of the most critical, issues in our consideration of sharing the gifts God has given to us. This is particularly true in a worldwide family which includes many people whose most basic needs of human survival are met, as well as many who struggle daily to meet those same needs.

Often gifts and needs are seen as opposites, as the two ends of a continuum. In this view, a need is a request or a question, and a gift is the answer. But this polarization leads to the false view that the world is made up of people with gifts and people with needs. If we believe as a matter of faith that all of creation is "gifted," that God has not created "ungifted" beings, then we must find another way to understand this relationship. For this belief implies that those who struggle for survival are no less gifted than those who have abundance. What is the difference between them? The difference is that some have the means to nurture their gifts while for others that nurturing has been impeded.

From this perspective, need does not stand in opposition to gifts but is much more intimately related. Why do the hungry "need" food and the sick "need" healing? So that the gifts God has endowed them with are able to be nurtured and can in turn be "given." We could say that gifts "need" other gifts in order that they can in turn be given. What we call a "need" then, can in fact be seen as the cry of a gift that is trapped and cannot be fulfilled or given.

If gifts cannot be or are not given, they die or rot, and this is contrary to God's will. God has poured out gifts to all creation, not for death but for "abundant life." It is not only the hungry, the sick, and the poor whose gifts can be blocked and die. The gifts of those with abundance can also be trapped and cry out in need, and, if unanswered, these gifts also die. The biblical story of manna from heaven in Exodus 16 demonstrates just this. The manna was given by God in response to the hunger of the Israelites, but when some hoarded it, it "bred worms and became foul."

Need, then, can be seen as the vital link between gifts. It is always bi-directional. It is that which allows the resources and potentials of both the "giver" and the "receiver" to become gifts, to be given. To deny need, whether our own or that of the other, is to deny the gifts God has given.

Is Gift Sharing the Same As Gift Exchange?

Gift giving or sharing is often referred to in terms of exchange—an "exchange of gifts" or "gift exchange." This reflects the fact that gifts are relational and often initiate further gifts. In many cultural contexts an "exchange" of gifts is a means of formalizing a bond or relationship, a contract between two people or groups, which again emphasizes the relational and bonding power of gifts.

While the idea of "gift sharing" focuses our attention on the movement of gifts in response to need, the concept of exchange can lead to a stronger preoccupation with the gift itself rather than the relationship it builds and signifies. Exchange suggests an aspect of equivalency and balance, that a gift being given is more or less equal to a gift received. With such an emphasis our attention can shift to comparing the value of what is given to the value of what is received. We can thus become concerned with the transaction, with making sure that what we receive is in balance with what we give, and vice versa. We lose sight of a gift being the response to a need.

This subtle shift to being preoccupied with the respective value of gifts is a movement away from a theological and needs-related understanding of gift, and toward commercial exchange. Commerce plays an important role in the daily lives of nearly all of us, but it is different from, and should not be confused with, gift sharing. This difference can be seen clearly by looking at a biblical story.

Luke 15:11-32 gives the account of the lost (or "prodigal") son. At the beginning of the story, the son asks his father for the portion of the father's wealth that would eventually belong to the son through inheritance, and the father complies. When the son returns home, having squandered his inheritance, the father showers him with gifts: a warm welcome, a feast, clothing, and a ring.

Thus, the father twice gave gifts to his son. The first occasion is essentially a "transaction"; the preoccupation was with value, what the son rightfully "deserved." Verse 12 says that the father "divided his property between them," showing a clear focus on the value of the goods themselves. But the second gift-giving of the father is quite different. Here there is no question of equivalency and no focus on value. Indeed, the scandal of the event, which the elder son fully appreciates, is that the gifts of the father have no relationship to "deserving," to "justice," to reciprocity. Rather, the father's gifts are moved by need. And any parent will readily understand that it is not only the physical need of the son which motivates the father. Verse 20 says that when the father saw the son coming he was "filled with compassion." What was this compassion if not the father's "need" for his son's return?

Again, the point is not that commerce or exchange is bad and that gift sharing is good. Both have their place, but it is important that we understand the difference. Gift sharing is not about giving or receiving value; it is about using our gifts for the health of the body as a whole.

Do We Have An *Obligation* to Give Gifts?

In many cultures some degree of gift-giving and sharing is considered an obligation. For example, in many "traditional" societies it is considered an obligation to give hospitality, especially in the form of food, to visitors, or to share food with needy members of the community, or to give gifts on particular occasions such as marriages, initiations, and deaths. Often there are sanctions which make it very difficult for individuals to accumulate wealth. These obligations are based on a fundamental understanding that the gifts of an individual belong to the community as a whole.

Many religions reinforce the idea of obligatory giving, both to God and to other human beings. Sacrifice is one expression of this; another is the giving of alms, which for the ancient Israelite as well as for the modern Muslim is considered an obligation. Christianity retained the ideas of giving tithes and of charity, but the obligatory aspect of tithes and charitable giving has gradually weakened over time. In the process, tithing and charitable giving have in many "Christian" societies come to be understood as good things to do, practices that brings honor and status to the giver, but that are essentially optional exercises.

Individualism and capitalism have played an important role in weakening the obligation to give. In an oversimplification we can see that individualism emphasizes individual choice rather than obligation, while capitalism requires the accumulation of wealth.

While the above can help us to understand the background to obligatory and voluntary giving, it does not answer the question of whether as Christians we have an obligation to give. We do not believe that there is any simple answer to this question. But it is perhaps helpful to acknowledge that the issue of biblical faith, and perhaps of religious faith in general, is not the question of what we are obliged to do, but rather what is God's plan, what is the Divine intention for human beings and the world in general.

From a biblical perspective there is no real dichotomy in terms of God's intentions from the Old Testament to the New. In both we can see God's purpose as the fullness or abundance of life, motivated by God's love for us. And this purpose is achieved through the giving of gifts. The two great gift stories of the Bible—the creation and God's giving of Jesus—model this understanding clearly. In a sense this understanding cuts across the question of obligatory versus voluntary giving. It is through sharing God's gifts that abundant life is possible. When we share our gifts we join in God's plan.

Peace, Justice, and the Sharing of Gifts

It should be clear, from our own experiences with gifts and gift giving in our families, our churches, our communities, and our cultures, as well as from what has already been said in these materials, that gift sharing is concerned with peace and justice in a most fundamental way. Gifts are universally used to demonstrate peaceful intent, or to solemnize peace agreements, or to ask forgiveness for wrong and to restore peace.

When we understand gift giving as the means to abundant life and closer relationships with others, we acknowledge the demands of justice and the fact that to refuse to share our gifts perpetuates injustice.

The justice that comes through sharing gifts is not primarily concerned with equality. If we understand justice primarily in terms of equality, we are continually inclined to reduce differences to sameness, to common denominators. Gift sharing, on the other hand, gives value to difference, recognizing the uniqueness of each person, each part of creation, each gift, and the need of each to be fulfilled and empowered. Difference, rather than equality, is sought out, given value, and preserved because each difference is seen as an essential part of the whole.

Likewise, the peace that comes from gift sharing is a dynamic rather than a static peace. While sharing gifts is fundamentally relational, it is not focussed on reaching a point of balance in a relationship, but on equipping and empowering both parties to use their gifts to build further interrelatedness among all people.

Summary of the Biblical Understanding of Gift Sharing

Following is a summary of the biblical principles which are important to the understanding of how and why we share gifts.

1. Biblical Faith Rests on Two Great Gift Stories

These are the story of creation, in which God gives humans life and a world to live in, and the story of Jesus, a gift of God to redeem the world.

2. All Gifts Come From and Belong to God

a. This is the foundation of everything we understand about gifts. It is based in our understanding of God as Creator.

b. The belief in a Creator God is common to nearly all religious traditions.

c. The primary biblical reference for this point is the creation account from Genesis 1. But there are claims throughout the Bible of the sovereignty of God. Psalms 24:1-2, for example, states that the world and all that is in it belong to God because God created it.

d. All of creation is interrelated; it is not just the result of random activity by God.

3. God Intends That Gifts Be Shared

a. We know this because of God's example. God's creative works—the universe and Jesus—take on meaning only through being shared. God gave Jesus out of love for the world (John 3:16).

b. God's plan for creation is based on interrelatedness and relationship. When gifts are used to respond to the needs of others, a relationship is built and reinforced.

4. All of Us Are Equitably Gifted by God

Though our gifts are all different, there is no hierarchy among them because they all come from God, and all are needed by the body. I Corinthians 12 makes this point most clearly.

5. The Purpose of Biblical Gift Sharing is the Redemption of Creation

a. Sin or wrong occurs when we choose not to, or are prevented from, sharing our gifts. "Not sharing" interferes with the relatedness which God intends. This means that it is wrong to keep one's gift to oneself, just as it is wrong to prevent someone else's gift from being expressed.

b. Paul says that the real test of gifts is whether they contribute to the common good and build up community (I Corinthians 12:7).

c. Through sharing we participate in building the interrelated world that God intends.

Additional Biblical Gift References

There are many, many biblical stories, references, and metaphors about gifts. Most of these illustrations can be used to emphasize the main points concerning biblical gift sharing. These are first, that *all gifts come from and belong to God*, and second, that *God's purpose in giving us gifts is that we share them in responding to the needs of others.*

Following are references to several biblical gift stories that congregations may find useful in exploring the biblical message about sharing gifts. These and other gift references can be studied in small groups. Some of the questions that can be asked are: What are the gifts in the story? Who received gifts; who gave gifts? What is the result of sharing the gifts? How are the gifts used?

1. The creation story of Genesis is the foundational gift story of the Bible. It emphasizes God as the source of all gifts. It also highlights the theme of abundant life as the purpose of God's creation. The final verses of Genesis 1 speak explicitly of creation as God's gift to humans and other species.
2. Jesus is also portrayed in terms of a gift given to us. Isaiah 9:6 speaks of a "son given to us," and John's gospel states "For God so loved the world that he gave . . . "
3. The stories of Cain and Abel in Genesis 4, and of Esau and Jacob in Genesis 25 and following, both include gift-giving as an important part in each story.
4. In Exodus 16 God provides the gift of manna from heaven to the hungry Israelites
5. In I Samuel 1, the child Samuel is given by God to Hannah, and Hannah in turn gives Samuel to God's service.
6. The story of Elijah and the widow in I Kings 17 revolves around gifts given and returned.
7. In Matthew 2 the wise men bring gifts to Jesus.
8. The story of the woman who gave the gift of anointing to Jesus, and Jesus's return gift to her, is told in Luke 7.

The Global Family

by Ofelia Garcia de Pedroza, Gift Sharing Facilitator, Mexico

As we think about sharing gifts in the context of the global church, the image of *family* is often used. This image suggests that each member has different gifts and abilities, as well as different roles and functions. The structure of the family should provide all members with a secure setting in which to exercise their gifts for the benefit of all who form part of the family. As one part of the global church family participating in global gift sharing, we can enrich each other with our diversity of gifts.

As we observe the reality of family in our different societies, we see that the family has always existed as the base of social organization, and it continues to be part of the essential needs of people. It is in the family where people find their points of reference, their spiritual and material space, and their identities. Even today when families find themselves threatened by migration, the aging of the population, the dissolution of marriages, or war, families are of vital importance for the reconstruction of society. Family is an important biblical metaphor to understand the life and mission of the church.

At the same time, we can't ignore that in different countries, and even in different regions of the same country, there are diverse cultural expressions of family. And while these variations form part of a great richness to share, they also present us with traditions, customs, and habits which we assume from birth to be correct, but which in fact may not be healthy and can stand in the way of sharing gifts.

In a community in my country there is a custom that families sell their daughters for cash while they are young. It doesn't matter whether the girls agree; they are not even asked. This may sound like an exaggerated example. But although this is not practiced in Christian communities, as I have presented this program in different regions of Mexico I have observed that many people still base patriarchal domination on the Bible. This results in structures which oppress women and encourage phrases like : " . . . women should be silent," ". . . I do not permit women to . . .," ". . . women cannot be in front, cannot minister, cannot, cannot. . . ."

These observations lead us to ask how we can better understand the biblical concept of family and apply it in a more positive way, to discover, recognize, and empower the gifts of each member of the global family. It would be very valuable to review carefully whether our cultural understandings of family fit within the biblical perspective, and above all within the example of Jesus.

In the New Testament the concept of family is expressed mainly in terms of stewardship (*oikos/oikía* Acts 16:15; 1 Corinthians 1:16) and of responsibility (*therapeia* Matthew 24:45; Luke 12:42). Family in the Bible is defined through a wide range of relationships. When Jesus talked of family, he did not just refer to our modern concept of nuclear family, but rather he understood all those who respond with fruits of genuine repentance and faithfulness to God to be part of the family. Jesus thus provided a new sense of what it means to be family, and its value is found in the context of the Reign of God (Mark 3:31-35; 10:28, 31).

The Christian or church family has more to do with the quality of common life than with specific structures and defined functions. The nuclear family is defined more by the demands and limitations of a secular materialistic society than by Christian ideals. The ideal that we find in the New Testament is considerably more inclusive; it defines family as a new structure which includes those whom society rejects. Belonging to the family of Jesus are people of various social classes, diverse political ideologies, and even women of dubious reputation.

In contrast to his contemporaries, Jesus used the family to explain the character and mission of the messianic community, in the process filling the family image with authentic meaning. He taught his followers to pray to his *Father* in the same way he prayed—with a surprising intimacy, calling him "*Abba*" (Mark 14.36, Romans 8:15, Galatians 4:6). In this family, hierarchies based on supposed relative value or personal honor do not exist. The great ones, those of "higher authority," must be servants of the others. The differences (gifts, abilities, resources) among the members of the family are functional and serve to enrich the common life.

In view of this new image of family which Jesus gives us, it would serve us well, when we think of sharing gifts within the global family, to elevate only those values of our cultures which contribute to developing relationships, and that conduct which reflects an intimate relationship with Christ.

It is my view that the Christian family, the global family, has more to do with the quality of common life than with fixed cultural structures and functions. It involves learning to be an actual community in the middle of a world that is increasingly interconnected. Such a community promotes unity amid diversity and shares the gifts of those who have more with those who have less, in a spirit of true solidarity and love. It is inspired by Jesus, who being rich made himself poor and gave gifts to us—women and men!—in order to be a visible Christian community today.

May the guidance of the Holy Spirit help us to discover new forms of solidarity through living out this understanding of family, welcoming especially those who have been excluded, as we advance together toward the Reign of God.

About the Authors

Paskisa K. Tshimika is from Kajiji in the Democratic Republic of Congo. Since 1993, he and his wife, Linda, have been parents to three children of Pakisa's deceased brother.

Pakisa is a graduate of Fresno Pacific University. In 1976, just three weeks before he was to start medical school in Lyon, France, he was critically injured in a traffic accident in which he suffered numerous severe traumas.

His disability led him to choose public health administration as a career; he received his doctorate in public health from Loma Linda University in southern California.

For several years Pakisa served as Program Director for Africa and Director for Social Ministry for Mennonite Brethren Mission and Service International. Today he works as Associate Executive Secretary for Networks and Projects for Mennonite World Conference.

In 1999 the Tshimikas moved to Fresno, California, where they currently live.

Tim Lind was born in Scottdale, Pennsylvania. He is married to Suzanne Hilty and together they have six children, three of whom are adopted.

Tim has been involved in church-related international relief and development work, primarily in Africa, since 1968. With his family he has lived and worked in Congo, Madagascar, and South Africa.

He is a graduate of Goshen College, Goshen, Indiana, has studied at Associated Mennonite Biblical Seminaries in Elkhart, Indiana, and is currently enrolled in a Masters program in Religious Studies at the University of South Africa.

The Linds live in southern Michigan.